THE PRUDENTIAL STAFF AND THE GREAT WAR

THE PRUDENTIAL STAFF AND THE GREAT WAR

Compiled by H. E. Boisseau

1938

The Prudential Assurance Company Limited

Holborn Bars

LONDON

Sir Edgar Horne, Bart., Chairman of the Company

CONTENTS

FOREWORD

by Sir Edgar Horne, Bart.

In deciding to publish this record, the Directors were moved only by their affection and pride in the activities of those of their comrades who took part in the Great War, and by a desire that those who serve the Company in the future may know something of the loyalty and devotion which inspired the Staff during that dark period of trial.

The Directors are well aware that innumerable other companies and public concerns could publish similar records; but some people at home and many abroad do not appreciate the part played in the Great War by these companies and their staffs.

INTRODUCTION

A YOUNG man entering the service of the Company in, say, 1920 would have discovered little about his colleagues to indicate that scarcely a year before they had been soldiers, sailors or airmen, fighting in the grimmest war the world had yet known. A curious reticence concerning their soldiering was noticeable ; a desire to forget the four years behind them and absorb themselves once more with the pursuits and ambitions of ordinary business men.

Now and again the young man might hear a story of the trenches, told in a matter-of-fact way with that understatement characteristic of those civilian soldiers. On the whole, however, they kept their experiences to themselves. But despite their reticence, their desire to forget the War, every one of them was marked with a common stamp, an assurance and a dignity as of men who had passed through an ordeal and had not been found wanting.

And now, twenty years after the War ended, we have tried to tell the history of those men. This is their book in which as far as possible they tell their own stories. But there are few stories compared with the number of Prudential men who served in the forces. Our hope is that the letters and experiences printed in this book may be typical of all the letters and experiences. We believe they arc, because in other aspects of life the articulate few speak for the inarticulate many.

Perhaps it may be asked : Why write the book at all ? The answer is that the time will come when all Prudential men who served in the War will have retired. Is it not fitting that the new generation should know something of what they did in the War ? Their record is a proud one, no less than that of England as a whole.

There is in these pages no effort 'To point a moral or adorn a tale', but a history, all too incomplete, of Prudential people in a time of national crisis. To those men and women who fought and endured and died this book is dedicated.

It was with these thoughts in mind that Sir Edgar Horne, Chairman of the Company, suggested that such a record should be compiled.

There were obvious difficulties to be faced. Of the 9,161 men who served many had passed away and some had left the service of the Company. Only about half of this total were available to be approached for any kind of story at all. And of those with whom it was possible to make contact, only a comparative few were able to recall their experiences in great detail.

Nevertheless, by means of a general enquiry, and through reference to the files of the *Prudential Bulletin* and the *Ibis Magazine*, a definite history has emerged, which those who served will read with interest and which, it is hoped, will make an appeal to an even wider public.

It must, however, be impressed upon the reader at the outset that this is not a complete Prudential history of the War so far as individual members of the staff are concerned. If every man's war record was set out in full several volumes would be necessary. But the information is not now available.

An endeavour has been made to present a narrative which covers as broad a field as possible. Throughout the book the names of the men and women involved have been quoted because the main interest lies in the fact that it is a personal Prudential history. The names have come into the narrative in a fortuitous manner ; that is to say, when it so happens that a story is available which fits into the narrative at the point required, that story has been given and the name quoted.

In conclusion I should like to express my thanks for the valuable help received from Messrs. R. W. Barnard, P. C. Hughes, V. G. Taylor, A. H. Windsor and H. J. Young, who kindly assisted me in putting the history into the final form in which it now appears.

H. E. BOISSEAU

AUGUST 4TH, 1914

IN August, 1914, the Staff of the Prudential were going about their peaceful occupations. Some were holiday-making. Out of the blue came the bombshell of war and the whole course of their lives was altered. Men who had believed themselves destined to lead useful but unexciting lives suddenly found themselves transported over the world to take part in adventures which, for them, had previously been found only in the pages of books. The year 1919 saw the resumption of the normal round of life, at least for some. But the experiences of those four years bit deep into the hearts and minds of the men who endured them. Now more than twenty years have passed. During the first 'after-the-War' years the general feeling was 'Let us forget'. The only way to regain a normal outlook was to inhibit the memories of those war years. Gradually this attitude changed and there came a spate of war books in which were set out in lurid detail all the horrors which men wanted to forget. That period, too, passed and we have now, perhaps, reached a stage when it is possible to take a dispassionate view grown out of experience and mellowed by time.

And so the story of how the Staff of one of the great business institutions of the Empire stood up to the shock of war is given. Writing it so long after the event has both an advantage and a disadvantage: the advantage that we see the War in a truer perspective and the disadvantage that much cannot be included that should be included because in the passing of time many who took part are no longer with us.

Nevertheless, the fact remains that there is no permanent record at present other than the Roll of Honour, which gives the names, regiments, and so forth, of all those who served. Some record of the human story lying behind this list of names should be made. Here, then, is the story for future generations to read.

THE OUTBREAK OF WAR

It was at eleven o'clock on the night of August 4th, 1914, when the British ultimatum to Germany expired. Winston Churchill, writing of what took place in a room in the Admiralty, said : 'Along the Mall from the direction of the Palace the sound of an immense concourse singing " God Save the King " floated in. On this deep wave there broke the chimes of Big Ben ; and as the stroke of the hour boomed out a rustle of movement swept across the room. The war telegram which meant " Commence hostilities against Germany " was flashed to the ships and establishments under the White Ensign all over the World. . . . The entry of Great Britain into war with the most powerful military Empire which has ever existed was strategically impressive. Her large fleets vanished in the mists at one end of the island. Her small army hurried out of the country at the other. . . . These two movements, actuated by the truest strategy, secured at once our own safety and the salvation of our Allies. The Grand Fleet gained the station where the control of the seas could be irresistibly asserted. The Regular Army reached, in the nick of time, the vital post on the flank of the French line.'

Now although to the majority of our people the War came as an unpleasant shock, those in authority were not taken by surprise and England was ready. When we say that England was ready, we simply mean that in many directions preparations had been made, and the preparation made by those associated with the Prudential must be our first consideration.

OUR VOLUNTEER FORCES

More than fifty years ago the late Sir Henry Harben, Chairman of the Company, made a speech in which he expressed the hope that members of the Staff would join the Volunteer Forces, and the Directors and Management of the Company have always encouraged the Staff to take up military service in their spare time.

There are still many of the Staff who remember the volunteer days prior to the South African War. At least one of our Staff was a trooper under Lieut. Winston Churchill in the Oxfordshire Yeomanry. These men were ready when the call to arms sounded in the later

1 H.E. Miller
2 E.S. Norton
3 E.E. Withall
4 P.A. Hemsley
5 J.C. Brown
6 A.E. Pratt
7 G.M. Taylor
8 H.G. Admans
9 J.S. Forrest
10 C. Nightingale
11 G.L. Andrews
12 P.C. Hughes
13 W.H. Sheehan
14 F.H. Wrigley
15 C.V. Manning
16 L. Pulsford
17 C.H. Toy
18 T.M. Bulley
19 H.C. Gravatt
20 E.P. Baxter

21 W.N. Hough
22 B. Humphries
23 H.G. Beale
24 A.F. Holman
25 H.B. Watkins
26 C.L. Rayment
27 W. Mortimer
28 H.D. Lidbury
29 E.H. Crease
30 H.G. Yearsley
31 W.W. Kelsey
32 D.T. Wood
33 H.J. Ockelford
34 E. Duval
35 J.W. Waterer
36 C.L. Jefferson
37 F.G. Taylor
38 W.T. Bendall
39 R.G. Lovelock

40 L.W. Berridge
41 H.W. Perkins
42 H.J. Young
43 R.H. Taylor
44 H.B. Owen
45 H. Humphreys
46 H.H. Morrison
47 M. Foulger
48 F.W. Lewis
49 A.V. Beechener
50 S.T. Lyon
51 E. Spencer Smith
52 F.G. Driskell
53 W.H. Russell
54 A.L. Coombes
55 W.E. Merrill
56 W.C. Burch
57 C.E. Nott
58 E. Ellis
59 J.H. Gunn

60 A.J. Simmonds
61 A.F. North
62 P.A.E. Wild
63 D.C. Abbott
64 L.C. Warren
65 T.F. Lawrence
66 W.T. Dawson
67 G.P. Simmonds
68 L. Criswick
69 W.T. Ritchie
70 E.J. Findlay
71 W.H. Hunnex
72 F.V. Simmons
73 A.H. Sudell
74 A.H. Windsor
75 F.H. Garraway
76 H.E. Egleton
77 A.E. Trembath
78 C. Beresford

79 Sir Thomas Dewey
80 A.J. Dart
81 H.W. Drake
82 F.E. Smith
83 F.C. Hammant
84 J.N. Shine
85 B.H. Cooper
86 C. Hopping
87 W.F. Symons
88 P. Creswick
89 G.F. Burnell
90 J.G. Hay
91 G.H. Davies
92 W.T. Copp
93 G. Kaines
94 W.J. Foster
95 H. Harrold
96 C.V. Smith
97 A.J. Miller
98 N. Kemp

99 E.V. Reading
100 E. Kemp
101 R.R. Leish
102 C.B. Yardley
103 W.H. Cullen
104 G.G. Crowe
105 F.T. Moth
106 A.H. Sabin
107 H.J. Debenham
108 T.P. Gurney
109 W.M. MacLeod
110 P.R. Harding
111 H. Sheppard
112 H.E. Brown
113 A. Griffiths
114 A. Rawlinson
115 A.H. Fountain
116 S.W. Moore
117 F. Izod

Members of the Chief Office Staff serving at the time of the Royal Review, 1913

months of 1899 and the C.I.V.s left for South Africa, to be fêted in London when they returned. Many Prudential men saw active fighting in South Africa under very difficult conditions.[1]

Mr. R. J. Bennett, for instance, tells us that during a fight in which his squadron (B Squadron, Imperial Light Horse) were engaged, thirty men out of seventy were killed and the others were, practically without exception, wounded.

Not a few of our men were mentioned in dispatches and one of them, Mr. A. E. Trembath, was awarded the Distinguished Conduct Medal and promoted to the rank of Lieutenant on the field.

There followed from 1902 a period of peace in which the Volunteer Force was regarded by the public with greater interest. Then came Lord Haldane's great reorganization of 1908 when the Auxiliary Forces became known as the Territorial Force.

We get a good idea of one aspect of the Territorial activities of the Prudential men on the eve of the War from the photograph taken of those of the Chief Office Staff who were serving at the time of the Royal Review of July, 1913. It is noticeable in the photograph that the majority had become N.C.O.s and that only a few were officers. This was a new tendency after the Territorial Force came into being. In the old days most seemed to have preferred to remain in the rank of a private soldier.

Generally speaking the old Volunteers had no organization above that of a Unit (Regiment of Cavalry, Battalion of Infantry and so on). There was thus a number of Units with no superior command and no cohesion. The Territorial Force was designed to form a

[1] The following are the names of a few of the Prudential men whom we have traced as having served both in the South African War and the Great War. These men are all alive today.

W. H. Atkins
W. H. R. Baines
W. Baxter
R. J. Bennett
J. Boxall
E. R. Bunkell
J. Christie
H. F. Drake
P. Edwards
W. S. Elsdon
F. Feltham
O. F. Green
J. Grundon
G. W. Hackwell
J. E. Hall
T. L. Harris
W. Higgins
D. M. Hopping
W. H. P. Jennings
H. F. Lawson
W. McDonald
R. B. Newson
E. F. W. Nixon
E. S. Norton
H. W. Perkins
F. J. Phipps
H. W. Plumstead
G. J. H. Priestley
R. E. Preedy
J. Purves
P. Rocker
J. A. Smith
W. H. Sprankling
W. Stephen
J. Taplin
W. H. Timms
J. Watson
A. H. Windsor

complete fighting force and produce (although at first only on paper) fourteen Army Divisions and one or two Mounted Divisions complete in every detail. Each Division was raised and maintained in a separate geographical position in the kingdom.

Voluntary Aid Detachments were raised to fill the gap between the Divisional Royal Army Medical Corps and the Home Hospitals. Thus for the first time the Auxiliary Forces were in a position to take the field with the same completeness of arms and services as the Regular Forces.

Some Units went with the Regular Army for training, and some went on Army manœuvres.

THE V.A.D.s

The British Red Cross Society's scheme for Voluntary Aid Detachments was first brought to the notice of the Staff at meetings held at Chief Office on May 26th, 1910. The Chairman of the Company—at that time Mr. H. A. Harben—presided. The male Staff was addressed by a number of distinguished people, including the Lord Mayor and Lady Mayoress, the Director of the Territorial Forces and the Red Cross Society's Director for the City of London. A similar meeting was attended by the lady Staff and presided over by the late Sir Thomas Dewey. It was proposed to form detachments which would be fully trained in First Aid. At both meetings the proposals were enthusiastically received. In March, 1911, two detachments—the first to be raised in the City of London—were formed and submitted to the War Office for registration. The Commandant was Mr. Paul Creswick, the Medical Officer Dr. E. M. Light, and the Quartermaster Mr. W. H. Hunnex. Mr. F. V. Simmons was Hon. Secretary and classes were commenced in conjunction with the St. John's Ambulance Association for instruction in First Aid and Home Nursing.

In June, 1912, under Commandants Paul Creswick and W. F. Symons, a contingent of Officers and men of our two detachments paraded in Hyde Park on the occasion of King George V's inspection of the London Division of the National Reserve. The ceremony was attended also by Queen Mary and Earl Roberts. On July 3rd, 1913, competitions in First Aid were held in the Guildhall and our detachments competed for trophies. H.M. King George V held a further review of London Territorials in Hyde Park on July 5th of that year and the detachments were again represented. On the 30th of the following month a Field Day was arranged at Windsor and fifty ladies and thirty men attended. There was an inspection by General Sir Charles Knox, K.C.B., and Colonels Cross, Magill and Harrison.

The War Office conducted an inspection of the detachments at Chief Office on October 10th, 1913, and expressed satisfaction with their efficiency. At this time Mr. W. F. Symons became Quartermaster and Dr. Otto May Medical Officer. Dr. May arranged a course of lectures which were well attended.

On 20th June, 1914, a Field Day was held at Putney where the late Sir William Lancaster placed his cricket field at the disposal of the detachments. Two days later it was announced at a meeting at the Mansion House that 2,381 detachments had been formed throughout the country, comprising some 70,000 members.

WAR!

On August 2nd, 1914, a camp was arranged to take place at Lulworth Cove. The first of our men to arrive at the camp—an advance party—were given instructions to return to London. The main body were dismissed as they were about to entrain and told to await further orders.

August 4th was a Tuesday. To all appearances normal work was busily resumed after the Bank Holiday. Many serving Territorials were in camp with their Units, a few had completed the 1914 training and a very few were going later on. Then came the news that a state of war existed. Those in camp proceeded to effect the necessary changes from a peace to a war footing ; those not 'up' for training immediately reported themselves to their Headquarters to be hastily 'vetted' by the Medical Officer or doctor called in for the purpose, and their Units formed ; in the case of Army Reservists each went to his regimental depot. War had come. The Staff of the Company, the majority of whom were not Territorials, carried on with their work. But from the 5th onwards there was a steady exodus of men to join the Colours.

AUGUST 1914 TO DECEMBER 1914

THE Directors of the Company [1] decided to maintain the salaries of all the Staff who joined the Colours, and on August 12th the whole of the male Staff were invited to assemble in order that the Chairman of the Company might address them. Both Mr. T. C. Dewey (later Sir Thomas Dewey, Bart.) and Mr. A. C. Thompson spoke. There was a great expression of loyalty at this meeting which concluded with the singing of 'God Save the King'. It was then announced that over 500 of the Staff had already joined the forces. Subsequently the Staff was to be denuded of nearly all men of military age and the stern reality of war faced. In the early days it was rather the terror of the unknown which had to be met with a cheerful outlook.

THE IBIS MAGAZINE

In this narrative will be found many quotations from the *Ibis Magazine*. This is the official organ of the Prudential Clerks' Society. It first appeared in 1878 and has been published monthly for private circulation ever since.

The following extract appeared in the September, 1914, issue: 'It is surprising how rapidly we have become accustomed to conditions affecting our civil life which are entirely new. We have been deprived of banking facilities for days and we have 'carried on'. The Stock Exchange has been closed for weeks and we survive; we use the blessed word 'Moratorium' as though we had been familiar

[1] The Directors of the Company at the outbreak of the War were: Mr. T. C. Dewey, Chairman, Sir William Lancaster, Deputy Chairman, Mr. W. T. Pugh, Mr. T. Wharrie, Mr. W. E. Horne, Sir John H. Luscombe, Sir Philip S. Gregory, Dr. J. I. Boswell, Surg. Lt.-Colonel H. R. Odo Cross and Mr. F. Schooling. The General Manager was Mr. A. C. Thompson.

with it for years and even the red and black 'Bradburys'[1] have ceased to excite our curiosity. The Government have intervened to fix the retail price of certain commodities and we do not protest; a Prudential party returning from an outing in motor chars-à-bancs is turned out to walk, while the motors are appropriated for military purposes, and it is treated as a humorous adventure; and last but not least, by a grand conspiracy of splendid silence, the British Public is kept in ignorance of the most stupendous movements of our troops until the whole force is transported to a foreign shore, and we applaud.'

The following verses were printed in the same issue:

Comrades! young warriors! your country calls!
  Calls on the eve of War and its alarms;
Bids you protect her, and maintain her walls:
  To arms! To arms! To arms!

Comrades! of whom we may indeed be proud!
  Sons of those Eighteen-Sixty Volunteers;
Sons of those sires whom the heedless crowd
  Greeted with ribald cheers,

Until at last their chance of glory came;
  Britain had need of them. They asked no more
Beyond the right to win a meed of fame
  Far from old England's shore.

Be yours to follow—yours, the strenuous part:
  Yours not to hesitate nor reason why,
But just to do your duty and depart
  To fight—perhaps to die!

Vivat Prudentia! Prudentia, long life!
  Your hope and mine! And when, our troubles past,
God's Will is done, may He, through storm and strife,
  Return you home at last!

ENLISTING

So intense was the enthusiasm in those early days that some managed to enlist although under age, over age, and even failing to come up to physical requirements. We quote a few stories here, but

[1] At the outbreak of the War gold was in circulation and sovereigns and half sovereigns were in use. One-pound and ten-shilling notes were a great novelty at this time. These bore the signature of the Joint Permanent Secretary to the Treasury (Sir John Bradbury), hence the name 'Bradbury'. It is curious that today there are millions who have never even seen a gold sovereign.

it must be borne in mind that in this book we can only hope to recount an infinitesimal part of the experiences of the Staff as a whole. The few incidents we have been able to collect more than twenty years after the event are quoted as typical.

Mr. J. D. Ballantyne was 16 years and 10 months old when he joined up. His height at the time was below standard by half an inch and his chest measurement by one inch. All this was remedied with the kindly aid of the Sergeant at the medical examination, who accepted Mr. Ballantyne's age as 19, placed his hand between Mr. Ballantyne's head and the slide when he gave his height, and wound the tape round his thumb at Mr. Ballantyne's back when the Medical Officer took down the measurements. To go to the other extreme Mr. G. W. Carter was over 45 years of age when he enlisted.

Mr. G. D. Cover tried to enlist in September, 1914, but was rejected. He was rejected eighteen times. He tried every branch of the service and enrolled as a Special Constable in 1915. He finally enlisted on 4th January, 1917, and after ten days was promoted to Lance-Corporal. He held every non-commissioned rank. He was offered the rank of Regimental Sergeant Major in 1920 by his commanding officer if he would stay in the Army.

Mr. R. Davies, whose weight was only 7 stone 3 lb., was told by the doctor that he was more suitable for a jockey than a soldier—but after three efforts succeeded in joining up.

Mr. W. J. K. Davison, when he joined up at Epping, heard the Officer Commanding call for a volunteer with clerical ability. He offered and was accepted, and in due course filled up his own attestation papers. At the end of the War he filled up his own demobilization papers.

Mr. W. H. Caesley landed in France within twenty-four hours of enlistment.

Mr. R. C. Haxton was in the front line with the 1st Royal Scots in Ypres six weeks after enlistment.

Mr. W. H. Jessop, who joined the Company after the War, was at Brandon, Manitoba, Canada, when war was declared. He landed in England in April, 1916, a private in the 79th Battalion Canadian Infantry.

Mr. A. Smith tried to join up with a friend. His friend was passed and he was rejected. Mr. Smith gave the Sergeant half a crown, whereupon he was told to come back at 2.30 p.m. At 3 p.m. he was passed A 1 by another doctor.

On his enlistment Mr. R. J. Betteridge was stationed at Hounslow to look after recruits, and was in control, under a Quartermaster, of all civilian clothing of recruits and despatched between 20,000 and 30,000 parcels of clothing.

Mr. H. S. Thompson was, in the early days, a Recruiting Officer and the Directors allowed him to have his headquarters in Chief Office. On one occasion Mr. Thompson made a recruiting speech from the stage during a performance at the Holborn Empire. He was well received and, after the performance, there was a rush of recruits.

THE FIRST GUNS FIRED

Two Prudential men claim to have been with the first guns fired in the War, one with the first gun fired in the Navy and the other with the first gun fired in France.

Mr. T. Neuenschwander was captain of the gun team which claims to have fired the first shot of the War on the 5th August, 1914. He did not enter the service of the Company until after the War. He came home at the end of July, 1914, after about eight months on the West Coast of Africa and went aboard the *Lance* on the 31st July, 1914. At 11.30 p.m. on the 4th August, 1914, the *Lance* steamed out of harbour and met the German mine-layer *Königin Luise*, in the early hours of the morning, returning after laying her mines. The signal was sent for the *Lance* to investigate. The *Lance* went ahead of the flotilla and fired a blank shot, but the *Königin Luise* did not stop. Orders were given to fire at her. 'I loaded the gun', says Mr. Neuenschwander, 'and looked at the Captain, for I thought the ship was a passenger steamer. The gun was fired and the ship which I had thought was a passenger steamer opened fire with all her guns. The Captain worked round to leeward of her. We were then joined by the *Legion* and the flotilla came up. After firing for about two hours the mine-layer was sunk. We picked up about 50 survivors whom we took back to Harwich. This being the first day of the War there was no official place in which to put prisoners, so they were incarcerated in a small steamer. Next day we took on some oil and went to sea again.'

Mr. J. Sullivan left Ireland on the 15th August, 1914, with 'E' Battery, Royal Horse Artillery, 2nd Cavalry Division, arriving in France on the 17th August, 1914. He was in action at 10.45 a.m.

on the 22nd August, 1914, with No. 4 gun, ' E ' Battery, Royal Horse Artillery, when it fired the first shot of the British Expeditionary Force in France. This gun, which was used through the War and finally went to Germany, is now in the War Museum at Lambeth.

Both Mr. Neuenschwander and Mr. Sullivan still represent the Company—Mr. Neuenschwander in Scotland and Mr. Sullivan in Ireland.

In this connection the following is also of interest. On the 31st May, 1915, when the first Zeppelins raided the city, London guns were fired in defence of the capital for the first time since De Ruyter sailed up the Thames in 1667. Under Commander Halahan, R.N. (who was afterwards killed at Zeebrugge), Mr. H. J. May, another Prudential man, passed the order simultaneously by telephone to all London Gun Stations—' All stations—Open fire ! ' Mr. May, after receiving his commission, served in the North Sea 1915–16, in the Adriatic 1916–18 and in the Ægean, Marmora and Black Sea, 1918–19.

THE FIRST BATTLES

Immediately the Germans marched into Belgium the Belgians resisted, making a firm stand at Liege. As a result the German Army was ten days late in arriving at the French frontier. During this delay General Joffre had time to reorganize his troops and Britain to send over an expeditionary force of 100,000 men.

At Mons and Charleroi battles were fought in which the Germans were victorious. There followed the ' Retreat from Mons ' and the Allies were forced to retreat to the Marne. The Germans were now within sight of Paris. Then the tables were turned and, after being severely defeated at the famous Battle of the Marne (6th–10th September), the Germans were driven back to the Aisne. Here they formed a line parallel with the river and another battle was fought—the Battle of the Aisne (12th–17th September). The result, however, was indecisive and both sides ' dug themselves in '. This marked the beginning of trench warfare.

Mr. A. J. Sears landed in France on 12th August with the 3rd Division. He was in action at Mons on the 22nd and 23rd August, taking part in the subsequent ' Retreat '. He tells us, ' During the first day of enforced marching an English and French aeroplane chased and forced down a German "Taube", which was set on fire by a volley fired by our Platoon. I believe that was the first aircraft casualty of the War.' Mr. Sears was also in action at Le Cateau and in the Battles of the Marne and Aisne.

Mr. H. J. S. Neate landed in France on 13th August and served with the 4th Guards Brigade at Mons, the 'Retreat', the Battle of the Marne and the Battle of the Aisne.

Mr. A. R. Cross also was in the 'Retreat' and in the Marne and Aisne Battles.

Mr. V. H. Skipworth, too, has given his name as one of the 'Old Contemptibles'.

Mr. A. H. Boxwell was captured in the 'Retreat' and was a prisoner of war in Germany for four years, doing labouring work on farms in various districts.

Mr. A. Kirby landed in France on 10th August, 1914, and fought at Mons.

Mr. G. Howard, Mr. T. Woodward and Mr. J. Osbourne took part in the 'Retreat', the latter acting as a stretcher-bearer.

IN TRAINING

Here is a letter from Mr. R. B. Newson written on October 15th, 1914. Mr. Newson was then a Lieutenant in the Royal Fusiliers. Later he was to become a Captain and be awarded the Military Cross. He was destined to be wounded near Gaza and spend some time in a hospital in Cairo. But the future was, of course, unknown to him when he wrote this letter:

'Since mobilization orders were issued, my time has been very much occupied, and the work has been of a varied character. During the first two weeks I was with the Civil Service (Territorial) Regiment, and we slept at Somerset House, our daily routine being Breakfast, 7 a.m.; Parade for route march, 9 a.m. till 1 p.m.; Dinner; afternoon parade, 2.30, for Musketry instruction, and sometimes bathing parade at Westminster Baths; Tea at 4.30, after which we were free (with the exception of men detailed for guards, etc.) till 9.30 p.m. A fortnight of this, and we were marched to Stanmore, on the way to Bedmond, near St. Albans. We arrived at 6 o'clock on a Sunday evening, and lay down for the night in an open field, resuming the march the next morning. The companies were billeted (and still are, I believe) on farms, the billets being widely separated from each other.

The training there is fairly hard, the intention no doubt being to make everyone as fit as possible, and harden them to endure privations.

'The programme consisted of physical drill and running in the early morning; field training after breakfast and dinner; and rest after tea, except when night operations were the order.

'After about ten days of this I was gazetted as a Second Lieutenant in Lord Kitchener's New Army, and left Bedmond for Colchester, where I found a small party of P.A.C. men in the 10th Battalion, Royal Fusiliers. Before I had time to settle down there I was transferred for duty to the 8th Battalion, Royal Fusiliers, also at Colchester. Three weeks later we entrained for Shorncliffe, where we are now under canvas, awaiting the completion of the huts which are being built for our accommodation during the winter months near Sandling Junction.

'Folkestone is of course full of Belgian Refugees and wounded Belgian soldiers, and they are being dealt with by committees formed in the town. Many ladies and gentlemen are devoting their time to the work of finding homes for these poor people. Their position is indeed pitiful, for in addition to having no home, they have nothing with which to occupy their time, except it be to brood over the devastation of their country, and the losses which their brave army has sustained in the gallant effort to defend the country so dear to them.

'They are full of gratitude to the people who are looking after them, as well as to the British Army, which is doing its best to help them.'

THE LIGHTER SIDE OF DRILL

This amusing story is told by Mr. S. G. Thompson and we give it in his own words. It gives a picture of the early training in Kitchener's Army.

'Our Sergeant-Major was one of the old "Dugouts" who, in answer to his Country's call, had come back from retirement to train the boys for the big adventure; a short dapper man of about 5 ft. 4 ins. with a ruddy complexion and a stomach which had run to seed as a result of retirement.

'A number of squads, each in charge of a Sergeant (mostly new promotions) were drilled every morning on the square at Aldershot, and the Sergeant-Major strutted round expressing his disapproval in hearty fashion and most expressive language. Stopping before our Squad one morning and admonishing the Sergeant on the slackness of his men he proceeded to tell us in his best regimental style the correct way of moving off from the halt position when ordered to do so.

'"The rear rank man *always* follows his front-rank man," he bellowed, and, as I happened to be a rear-rank man, he singled me out for his demonstration. "*You*," he shouted; "what would *you* do if *your* front rank man marched off to Edinburgh?"

'Standing stiffly to attention and looking directly ahead like a good soldier I tried hard to act up to the best traditions of the Army and refrain from even blinking an eye. Whereupon the Sergeant-Major answered his own question. "Yes! Just what I thought. *You'd* follow 'im, you would." Then turning to the Instructor he roared, pointing at me with his cane, "Watch 'im, Sergeant—watch 'im. He looks silly devil enough to follow his front-rank man anywhere." Then turning on his heel he strutted away for a few paces, suddenly again turning towards us and roaring: "Watch 'im, Sergeant, or you'll have the job of sending an escort to Edinburgh to fetch 'im back. Yes! 'im and his b—— front-rank man as well."'

THE SPIRIT OF THE MEN

Two quotations from letters show the spirit of the Country at the beginning of the War. This from Mr. A. F. North of the London Scottish:

'We are in the first unit of the Territorial Army to be taken for service, so feel rather proud of it, and will endeavour to do our duty and show that Territorials are made of the same stuff as the Regulars,' and from Mr. Cyril Brown: '. . . it will be grand to have a pot at the Germans.'

Mr. North's was no vain boast. On November 8th, 1914, three months after he had written those lines, he made the supreme sacrifice. He had sailed for France with the 1st Battalion of the London Scottish and went through the historic charge on November 1st without receiving a scratch, but in the subsequent action on November 8th he was hit on the back of the head by a piece of shrapnel, and although he was apparently not badly injured and walked to the hospital, he died on the following day.

As far as Mr. Cyril Brown was concerned it is interesting to note that the Germans were very successful in having a 'pot' at *him*. He was wounded three times—at Festubert in 1915, at Ypres in 1916, and on the Somme in 1916. In September, 1918, he was awarded the Military Cross.

ALL MUST HELP

There was a 'leave-no-stone-unturned' spirit animating all at this time. This letter published in the *Ibis Magazine* is typical of the feeling of those left at home.

15th September, 1914.

DEAR SIR,

It was my privilege last week to witness a civilian drill at Salisbury House, and I was surprised to see the large number of men who contrived simple evolutions in a space scarcely larger than our rifle range.

I understand these men are not eligible for service either with the Territorials, or what to my mind is misnamed 'Kitchener's Army', but they believe that part of their leisure should be spent in obtaining a knowledge of military movements. Whilst the glorious exploits of our Forces in France give every hope of ultimate victory to the Allied arms, we are repeatedly warned by those in authority that we must take no chances, and it may be that in the event of the necessity occurring for the creation of further defence forces, the efforts expended by these men at Salisbury House and elsewhere will prove invaluable.

I believe, Sir, that among my colleagues there are many who notwithstanding the exigencies of our business are willing, indeed would gladly welcome the opportunity of renewing their acquaintance with or obtaining instruction in these matters. Small squads of P.A.C. men could, I feel sure, find spaces in this great building, and could devote *at least* two hours a week with this object in view.

There is another side to the question. The majority of us are probably unable to obtain the physical exercise which is admittedly beneficial to one's health, and the adoption of such a scheme therefore *may* prove to be of service to our country, and a certain advantage to ourselves.

P.A.C. men have been sent to the front. P.A.C. men are serving at home. P.A.C. men are helping the wounded. P.A.C. men are undoubtedly serving their country by remaining here at their work and, as our Chairman put it at that memorable meeting, 'seeing to it that the machinery of this National Institution continues to run smoothly'.

It is, Sir, in my opinion, also the duty of these last, who might be described as the Ibis Old Guard, to do their best to be prepared as far as they are able to march and shoot in defence of home if the necessity arises.

I am, Sir,
Yours faithfully,
EX-VOLUNTEER.

GRONINGEN, OCTOBER, 1914

'The menace to Britain'—we are now quoting from B. H. Liddell Hart's history of the War—'if the Channel ports fell into German hands, was obvious. It is a strange reflection that, inverting the German mistake, the British command should hitherto have neglected to guard against the danger, although the First Lord of the Admiralty, Winston Churchill, had urged the necessity even before the battle of the Marne. When the German guns began the bombardment of Antwerp on September 28th England awakened, and gave belated recognition to Churchill's strategic insight. He was allowed to send a Brigade of Marines and two newly formed Brigades of Naval Volunteers to reinforce the defenders, while the Regular 7th Division and 3rd Cavalry Division, under Rawlinson, were landed at Ostend and Zeebrugge for an overland move to raise the siege. Eleven Territorial Divisions were available in England, but, in contrast to the German attitude, Kitchener considered them still unfitted for an active rôle. The meagre reinforcement delayed, but could not prevent, the capitulation of Antwerp, October 10th, and Rawlinson's relieving force was too late to do more than cover the escape of the Belgian Field Army down the Flanders coast.

'Yet, viewed in the perspective of history, this first and last effort in the west to make use of Britain's amphibious power applied a brake to the German advance down the coast which just stopped their second attempt to gain a decision in the west. It gained time for the arrival of the main British force, transferred from the Aisne to the new left of the Allied line, and if their heroic defence at Ypres, aided by the French and Belgians along the Yser to the sea, was the human barrier to the Germans, it succeeded by so narrow a margin that the Antwerp expedition must be adjudged the saving factor.'

Several Prudential men joined the newly formed Brigade of Naval Volunteers. Here is an extract from a letter written from Groningen in Holland just after the event. The writer, Mr. A. G. Gowing, survived the War, but died in 1925.

'A week of active service and only three days in the trenches was indeed a short career; but it is at least some consolation to know that we have done "our bit" and a little for which we appear to have received more praise than we think was due to us.

'Personally I never expected to get away from Antwerp, owing to the numerical superiority of our enemy, and although we appear to have lost rather heavily, it certainly seems a miracle so many of us got away so well.

'During the whole of the week, October 4th, when we left Walmer Camp about 12 o'clock noon, until the following Saturday evening, when we were compelled to cross the Dutch frontier, I only secured about six hours' sleep, and the rations for the majority of us were unfortunately conspicuous by their absence.

'On the last day of our retreat, not having had any food for three days, we were forced to satisfy our hunger upon apples only, which we were obliged to "steal" from orchards as we passed.

'I am, however, very proud to think I have been permitted to fight side by side with the Belgians, who have without doubt suffered cruelly at the hands of the invaders.

'Many are the times during that week when I saw these brave little soldiers share their rations and water with us, even when going into the trenches themselves. They look upon us as the champions of their cause, and it will indeed be an everlasting shame to England if her manhood fails her in this her "blackest hour".

'You can, I am sure, form some opinion of our condition when we crossed the frontier, seeing that we completed our week's work with a forced march of 50 miles; all the while closely followed.

'Many of our fellows gave up and had to be left at the roadside, and I should, I am certain, have added one to their number, had I not been cheered along the way by my comrades.

'As interned men we are treated with every consideration that we can expect, but it takes a great deal to compensate for being a prisoner.

'We each have a small bed, upon which we sleep, dress, and in fact almost live—if such is living.

'We have, however, "to grin and bear it", looking for brighter times in the future, and contenting ourselves with the news of passing events which gets through to us.'

Mr. H. G. Bromhead also was interned in Holland following the fall of Antwerp. He spent over four years in the Internment camp at Groningen. The men were housed in huts, each of which accommodated roughly 450. Camp life was extremely monotonous, for apart from a compulsory route march daily there were no fixed duties, and it depended on the individual himself how far his time was occupied. Sports and amateur theatricals were arranged. Latterly Mr. Bromhead was allowed a month's leave in England on parole. On the return journey he was on board the s.s. *Copenhagen* when she was torpedoed off the Dutch coast.

MESSINES, NOVEMBER, 1914

We have been allowed to publish part of a letter from Mr. W. H. Petty, written to his wife on the 2nd November, 1914, which gives a vivid picture of the London Scottish in action at Messines.

'. . . We went into action the day before yesterday . . . We had to take a trench, and to do so we had to cross a large potato-field that was absolutely swept by shrapnel; they had the range to a T, also snipers on it, to say nothing of a Maxim gun. We crawled along a ditch, which was full of nettles; it was hard work crawling about a quarter of a mile in our overcoats and with our packs. We next crossed a field, running in single file, and gained the trench, which was five feet deep, but we couldn't open fire as they had the range of this trench also, and simply swept it with their guns, shrapnel and lyddite, and trained another Maxim on it, so we had absolutely no alternative but to retire, which we did as quickly as we could. . . .

'We dug ourselves into trenches for the night in anticipation of an attack at dawn, right on a road, and of course no sleep and no food except a few biscuits. We have had no sleep for about three days now. When dawn broke we kept sniping off any stray Germans that came our way, but suddenly along the top of the road came hundreds and hundreds of them to our rear and we were in a trap. We tried hard to beat them back, as Findlay and Jock Anderson, two of our good shots, lay in the middle of the road and opened fire on them, but there were only about forty of us, so it was hopeless, and the order was given to retire with them only about fifty yards behind. . . . I had to run right across a ploughed field right up to the tops of my boots in mud, with twelve of them in one corner potting at me. . . . I now stand with nothing in the world except my clothes, my rifle and ammunition, but thank God I am alive. Only about twenty of us have got through to here; we joined in with the Regulars and fought a rearguard action as we kept retiring, and at last I think we held them. . . .'

Two other Prudential men, namely Mr. P. A. E. Wild and Mr. G. H. Swain, who were also serving with the London Scottish, were both wounded in this battle on the 31st October. Mr. Wild contracted pneumonia and pleurisy after exposure in trenches at Givenchy in the following February. He returned to England in March and was discharged as unfit in April, 1915. Mr. Swain was destined to travel yet further afield and served on the North-West Frontier, India, in the Aden Machine Gun Corps.

CHRISTMAS DAY, 1914

On Christmas Day, 1914, English and German troops left their trenches to exchange greetings and gifts. Here is a description of what happened, written by Mr. W. R. M. Percy of the London Rifle Brigade:

'We had rather an interesting time in the trenches on Christmas Eve and Christmas Day. We were in some places less than a hundred yards from the Germans, and we talked to them. It was agreed in our part of the firing line that there should be no firing and no thought of war on these days, so they sang and played to us several of their own tunes and some of ours, such as "Home, sweet Home" and "Tipperary", etc., while we did the same for them. The regiment on our left all got out of their trenches and every time a flare went up they simply stood there, cheered and waved their hats, and not a shot was fired on them. The singing and playing continued all night, and the next day (Christmas) our fellows paid a visit to the German trenches, and they did likewise. Cigarettes, cigars, addresses, etc., were exchanged, and everyone, friend and foe, were real good pals. One of the German officers took a photo of English and German soldiers arm in arm, with exchanged caps and helmets.

'On Christmas Eve the Germans burnt coloured lights and candles along the top of their trenches, and on Christmas Day a football match was played between them and us in front of the trench.

'They even allowed us to bury all our dead lying in front, and some of them, with hats in hand, brought in one of our dead officers from behind their trench so that we could bury him decently. They were really magnificent in the whole thing, and jolly good sorts. I have now a very different opinion of the German. Both sides have now started firing, and are deadly enemies again. Strange it all seems, doesn't it?'

Strange indeed. This was to be Mr. W. R. M. Percy's last Christmas Day. On April 28th of the following year, while under a heavy bombardment in the trenches near Ypres, he was killed by a shrapnel bullet.

Mr. W. V. Mathews of the Queen's Westminster Rifles also describes the Christmas incident:

'We came out of the trenches on Boxing morning after spending a most remarkable Christmas. On Christmas Eve we got a bit "rowdy", and shouted messages over to the Germans who occupied the trench opposite us, and we agreed on both sides not to fire at each other on Christmas Day. We got out of our trenches in the morning and played football, and then went out in front and walked over to meet them. We then shook hands and exchanged souvenirs with each other. They could talk English, and it gave me an opportunity of exercising my little German. You will no doubt admit that this experience was most extraordinary during such a war as this. These men seem very friendly, and want the war to end. . . .'

And here is Mr. C. L. Jefferson's version of the incident:

'Soon after we arrived in France I left the transport section and joined the company, so that I have been into the trenches with the rest of our fellows. As you say, the transport section remains in the rear, their work is to bring our rations and mail to the Headquarters, which as a rule is about a thousand yards behind the trenches. We then send a party out from the trenches to fetch the rations, etc. Of course all this work is done at night. Getting in and out of the trenches is one of the most dangerous jobs, the Germans are always sending up flash-lights; when these go up one has to fall flat on the ground, which very often is not quite so dry as High Holborn.

'I expect that you read in the papers about the Christmas truce. Our company was in the trenches at Christmas and it was an experience which I should not like to have missed.

'On Christmas Eve things went on as usual (one poor fellow was shot through the head a few yards away from me) until dusk came, when suddenly all rifle-fire ceased and the Germans sang carols to us until the early hours of the morning.

'When daylight came we all got out of the trenches and met the Germans half-way, when an exchange of souvenirs took place. I changed a pot of jam for two German cigars, which were a gift from the Kaiser to his troops.

'We kept this truce up for about a fortnight, although the artillery took no notice of it and killed six of their men, and their artillery killed two of ours. However, this did not seem to affect the feeling between both sides, for when New Year's Eve came we had a greater time than ever.

'The Germans hung Chinese lanterns along the top of their trenches, only fifty yards in front of us, and then they entertained us for several hours with a fine band. Their programme included "Now thank we all our God", and "Home, sweet Home", but we were most surprised when they played "God Save the King".

'They warned us that they were going to fire a "feu de joie" at 11 o'clock, so that we all had to stand to in case of an attack. When 11 o'clock came there was a terrific report which, although we were expecting it, made us all jump. However, they continued to entertain us with their music. One of them brought us over a bottle of wine and a box of cigars; he was as drunk as he possibly could be.

'In the morning we made arrangements with them to bury some dead cows, which had been lying between the trenches for weeks; it was very funny to see English and Germans working side by side. One of the Germans was a porter from Victoria Station, and another had played football for a Nottingham team.'

No doubt many Prudential men took part in this fraternization, and amongst them we know to have been Messrs. W. E. Hegarty, W. Mortimer and S. C. Ashdown. Mr. A. J. Goldsmith took part in a similar incident in December, 1916, near Combles.

THE OUTLOOK AT THE END OF 1914

The *Ibis Magazine* Editorial at the end of each year of the War period is most interesting, as it shows the reaction of the people at home to each phase. It will be noticed from the following quotation that a speedy end had been foretold, but now all attempts at prophecy were to be abandoned.

'After three months of War on a prodigious scale without any decisive issue on either side,' says a writer, 'we begin to wonder how long it is possible for such a state of things to continue. Those who rashly foretold that the end would be reached within this period will have to make their calculations afresh, or more wisely abandon all attempts at prophecy.'

THE MANAGER WRITES TO THE MEN ON SERVICE

At Christmas, 1914, the Manager sent a letter to every man on active service. We have been able to secure one of the original letters and a reproduction of it is given on the following pages. With the letter was sent a gift of chocolate from the Directors and Principal Officers of the Company.

PRUDENTIAL ASSURANCE COMPANY, LIMITED.

COMMUNICATIONS ON THE SUBJECT OF THIS LETTER SHOULD BE ADDRESSED "THE GENERAL MANAGER."

TELEGRAMS – "PRUDENTIAL HOLBORN LONDON."
TELEPHONE – "HOLBORN 6614" (6 LINES.)

HOLBORN BARS, LONDON, E.C.

Christmas 1914.

Dear

I want to convey to you on behalf of the whole Company, Directors, Officers and other Colleagues alike, our most hearty good wishes for your welfare.

We are proud of the response made by Prudential men to the call of the Country and our appreciation of the noble deeds performed by our Navy and Army is quickened and intensified by the knowledge that, in these Services, there are hundreds of Officers and men who have forsaken the relatively uneventful Prudential life and have offered, and in some cases given, their all in the Nation's Cause.

We are very confident that your

PRUDENTIAL ASSURANCE COMPANY, LIMITED. Sheet No.

2

conduct in attack or in defence will unceasingly prove worthy of the standards of duty, honour and efficiency which have always been maintained in our peaceful ranks: be sure that you are always in our minds and if in any way we can minister to your comfort or to that of any who may be dependent upon you, do not hesitate to acquaint us with the need.

You and your comrades are engaged in the destruction of the hostile and aggressive spirit of the enemy in order to ensure to the Nations, great and small, the opportunity, too long hindered and menaced, of promoting the Cause of Peace and Goodwill to which our thoughts turn longingly at this Holy Season.

We are sure you will take your full

PRUDENTIAL ASSURANCE COMPANY, LIMITED. *Sheet No.* ___

3

part in such operations as you may be privileged to share with this object in view and, never doubting the complete and early success of the Allied Forces, we look forward to the time when we may once more enjoy association with you in our commercial efforts for the advancement of National prosperity.

I have the pleasure to forward to you herewith a gift of chocolate from our Directors and Principal Officers in token of their interest in your welfare.

May all good fortune attend you

Yours Sincerely

A. C. Thompson

General Manager

1915: TRENCH WARFARE

MR. W. E. JONES, of the Queen's Westminster Rifles, writing from Maidstone early in January, 1915, mentions the departure of 250 men for France. He says, 'I should like to have said good-bye to the P.A.C. men, amongst whom were Agate, Purry, Waddington and Joyes.' It is interesting to follow the fortunes of these men.

William John Waddington was killed in action in the following February, carried to a Field Hospital by Purry.

Harold Agate was sent to France in 1915 and soon showed himself fitted for higher responsibilities, and his progress from Lance-Corporal to Captain was rapid. He was given the uncommon distinction of being commissioned in the regiment in which he served as a private, was highly regarded by his Commanding Officer, respected and admired by the men.

On the morning of the 14th April, 1917, Captain Agate led his men in an attack on the German lines in the Wancourt area, and was hit after advancing nearly a mile. His batman carried him to a shell-hole about 200 yards from the enemy, and with extraordinary ability and devotion attended Captain Agate and two other men for thirteen hours, dressing their wounds and feeding them with the little food they had with them, under continuous fire from the German snipers. The batman finally decided to go for stretcher-bearers, who, weary as they were, made attempts to find Captain Agate, but they failed to discover the particular hole, a difficult matter in the dark in 'No Man's Land'. The line was evacuated just then, and it would seem that Agate died from exposure, as another regiment advancing at a later date found and buried his body. Purry finished as a Lieutenant and returned safely. Joyes also survived, being ultimately promoted to the rank of Captain. In 1917 he was in France with the Leicestershire Regiment and spent 1918 and 1919 in India serving on the North-West Frontier and in Baluchistan. W. E. Jones served throughout the War in France and Belgium until demobilized in 1919.

IN THE TRENCHES

Extracts from a letter, written by Mr. F. L. Parker, give an excellent idea of life in the trenches. Mr. Parker was wounded at the 2nd Battle of Ypres early in 1915, but ultimately returned home safely.

'. . . A small party with a surgeon were "told off" for the place in which we now are. It is the ruins of a house just behind our trenches and is surrounded by a barricade of sand-bags. We have dug-outs in which it is just possible to lie down or sit up. It was a rotten walk getting here. We carried full packs, including a blanket. It was pouring heavens hard and as black as ink. The poor fellow in front of me fell over twice. On arriving here, two fellows were put on sentry go, and the rest turned in and tried to sleep. My hours were from 1.30 a.m. to 3.45, and it was cold, although fortunately the rain had stopped. We are cut off all day from anybody else, because of the danger of being shot, so we have to get the rations at night. The second night there, three of our men went off to the trenches to get our rations. As they were so long away I was sent with another man to look for them. At the start I fell into two shell-holes filled with water, and finished by falling into the communication trench. We had to drop every few yards as the Germans were sending up a constant stream of flares. We found the others waiting for the food, which had not arrived. Yesterday I did three journeys in the gloaming to a wood near by, to get food for our party. Sleeping in this dug-out is not all honey, as it is so cramped, and, being so long, my legs stick out at the end and recline in an inch or two of mud and water. But what's the odds—I manage to sleep splendidly!'

A DESCRIPTION OF A DUG-OUT

This was written by Mr. G. J. N. Best—also early in 1915:

'. . . You may like to have more of an idea of what our dug-outs are like, as they form our home for a quarter of our time. The new ones we are having built in our trench have wooden floors and sides, with corrugated iron roofs, on which sand-bags (or rather canvas bags filled with mud and clay) are packed closely round the edges, with mould dug from the front of the parapet to fill up the centre. This makes it proof against shell splinters and shrapnel (I am glad to say our trenches have not been shelled so far). The size of our dug-outs is about 6 feet by 6 feet 6 inches, and 4 feet high. Then we improve on them ourselves, by putting up shelves (for accommodating our eatables), bracket for candle, etc., etc. In this we have to accommodate three men and one on guard, so that when we snug in together we are quite comfy and warm. At night, unless there is a very bright moon, we have listening patrols out, i.e., two men who go out in front of the trench, who listen and watch very carefully to prevent any surprise attacks. (We happen to be in a particularly quiet part of the line, and have not had anything in the nature of an attack since our regiment took over the trench.) We are turned out an hour before sunrise to "stand to", during which hot pea-soup and rum are served out. The day is spent in bailing and keeping the trench "respectable", and making little improvements of our own, and then in sleeping, reading, cooking, and eating, so at present you see we are not having such a bad time. At the end of our three days, as soon as the relieving company comes up, we file out and march back to "town" for our three days' recuperation.'

THE SECOND BATTLE OF YPRES, 22ND APRIL–8TH MAY, 1915

The 2nd Battle of Ypres is notable in view of the fact that it was in this battle that the Germans introduced poison (chlorine) gas. Amongst others from the Prudential who were engaged in the battle were:

L. G. J. Adams	H. J. N. Debenham	C. H. D. Pratt
F. A. Cobb	T. V. Fawell	W. L. Sadler
G. H. Davies	F. Izod	A. J. Simmonds
G. E. Daviss	H. B. P. Owen	P. M. Stephens

Mr. S. C. Ashdown, who also took part, saw the famous Cloth Hall burning.

Messrs. G. H. Davies and H. J. N. Debenham were sent down to Poperinghe to assist in making some of the first hastily improvised respirators for use against the gas.

Mr. G. J. M. Best was one of eighty-three survivors in a Battalion

THE LONDON RIFLE BRIGADE

Back row : P. D. Power, H. L. Wontner, W. J. Redway, H. W. Furrell, H. S. Bennett, F. Sawyer, D. J. Thomas, E. J. Robertson, C. W. Gates

Middle row : T. C. Jones, J. S. Watkins, W. Mortimer, H. D. Lidbury, W. F. Boaden, C. H. Bright, A. R. Paine

Front row: A. H. Heness, G. Fitzsimons, S. G. Richardson, H. W. Lewis, G. Cook, R. A. Bailey, J. T. West

of about eleven hundred after the battle. After one day in the reserve line following the retirement he led a relief party to Sergt. Belcher, who was awarded the V.C. Within a few hours of effecting the relief, however, Mr. Best was wounded and gassed.

Mr. A. G. Johnson tells us: '. . . the battery to which I belonged was far in advance of any other at the 2nd Battle of Ypres and the first to have experience of gas on 22nd April, 1915.'

A RED CROSS ORDERLY IN BELGIUM

The following letter, written by Mr. G. G. Crowe, who was a British Red Cross Orderly attached to the Belgian Army, is interesting as Crowe was destined to have varied experiences before the end of the War. In 1914 he was in France and in 1915 in Salonica. In April, 1916, he arrived in Mesopotamia and was attached to the Indian Army Expeditionary Force for the relief of Major-General Townsend at Kut. In December, 1914, Crowe and another orderly met the Prince of Wales (now Duke of Windsor) with whom they had a conversation. His Royal Highness allowed Crowe and the other orderly to travel to England in his steamer, although permission had previously been declined. Our colleague wrote:

'From the nursing point of view ward work is the most interesting, but my work is mostly out-of-doors. I spend my mornings looking after cows! I also go out a good deal in the motors, generally for stores, and when the fighting recommences we shall go up again to the front for wounded. One of the most interesting sights is to go to the station and see the train arrive from the front. Those who can walk help those who can't, and they all look fed up. The best tonic is a cigarette, which as a rule never fails to produce good effects. They dress the worst cases and send them on to our hospital, usually in the middle of the night. We expect to be full up and very busy when the fighting begins. Our great day is sending the wounded (all Belgians) to England. They tie all their belongings in a handkerchief and insist on looking cheerful so as to be told they are well enough to go. We have had a Zeppelin right over the hospital, but very little damage was done. We start work at 7.30 in the morning and go on until 7.30 at night. We sometimes play football after dinner and recently played against the French and *lost*! Our best player had to go to Boulogne for exceeding the speed limit with his motor in that city. We have a piano in our dining-room, and every evening when we dine (it is really the officers who dine) the best player in Belgium plays to us. We are expecting some Zeppelins to-night (Sunday) in fulfilment of a promise of the Kaiser's. Our favourite rumour is, "Ostend is taken"; it is served up fresh every week or so.'

THREE GALLANT GENTLEMEN

On May 9th, 1915, Lieut. Harold Thompson, the elder son of the then General Manager, was killed in action at Festubert, and the sympathy of the whole Staff went out to Mr. and Mrs. A. C. Thompson in their bereavement. On May 11th, 2nd Lieut. Edward John Findlay died after wounds received on the previous Sunday. He had taken part in the London Scottish action at Messines and of him, on that occasion, a comrade had written: 'Sergeant Findlay was marvellous in the trenches; he really saved all our lives and was congratulated by the Colonel. He was splendid.' At the outbreak of the War Findlay was 41 years old. He had seen service in the South African War and he might well have thought that his military responsibilities were over. But he responded to his country's call, rejoined his old regiment as a private soldier, and soon regained his former rank of Sergeant, commissioned rank being bestowed in recognition of his services under fire.

On May 26th Captain A. E. Trembath, D.C.M., was killed. Here the Nation and the Company lost a man with ability which many thought akin to genius. It is mentioned on page 3 that in the South African War he was awarded the Distinguished Conduct Medal for an act of conspicuous bravery. He never referred to any such incident in his career and seemed to resent any reference to it. He was shot whilst helping a wounded man. 'When I was by the stretcher helping to hold him up he recognized me and said, "How's the Company? Are they all right?" I told him they had got clear and he smiled up at me and said, "That's good".' This from a comrade with him when he died. He was a man who had loved his garden, and flowers from his children—'To our darling Daddy from his garden'—were sent to be placed on his grave. A cross in the burial ground at Festubert marks the grave of Allan Trembath, a gallant Englishman.

VOLUNTARY WORK ON MUNITIONS

In August, 1915, an interesting description was given by a Prudential man, whose name has been lost in the passing of the years, of voluntary Sunday munition work in England.[1] The writer described himself as an Old Artillery Volunteer and the idea of assisting in munition work attracted him. The responsibility of organizing the work in this particular factory at Dagenham had been taken over by members of the local Golf Club. Golf in this particular spot was dead and the members organized the workers who received payment and handed it to local hospitals. 'My "boss" informed me,' says this writer, 'that my work to-day is "milling centre-plates". Soon I am in the swing of the thing and the morning goes quickly.' Later he says, 'My day's work resulted in some fourteen hundred completed centre-plates which, my "boss" remarked, compared very favourably with the normal output. What is being done here is assuredly being done in many other places and should give undoubted assistance to the schemes of the Ministry of Munitions. The feeling of satisfaction experienced by the Volunteers goes without saying. I have seen staid elderly business men openly kissing the completed fuses they were handling.' Read twenty years afterwards those last lines seem a little foolish perhaps—but they do indicate the will-to-win sentiment which permeated the whole population at the time.

ON BOARD H.M.S. *PROSERPINE*

Meanwhile Prudential men were doing good work afloat. This is how Mr. B. H. Cooper writes in April, 1915. He was then a Paymaster Sub-Lieut., but eventually left the Service with the rank of Commander. We give the name of the ship although this was withheld at the time of writing.

'For several weeks H.M.S. *Proserpine* has been patrolling a broad and beautiful bay penetrating into the heart of an enemy country, hence there has not been any chance of dispatching mails and there probably will not be one until we return to port for coal. Our fresh provisions were exhausted some time since, and we have been revelling in such good old-fashioned sea fare as salt horse and hard biscuit, relieved by the luxury of a sardine occasionally, or a slice of tinned tongue, and washed down with lime-juice. Whenever and wherever

[1] I have since discovered that the writer is Mr. P. J. Hogston, the present Editor of the Prudential Bulletin.

anything in the nature of trenches or fortifications, troops or transports is observed, boom go the guns, the shells whiz, and the shrapnel (or lyddite) bursts. Bridges, railway rolling-stock, telegraph apparatus, etc., etc., are all considered fair fodder for cannon.

'We were sent away on this stunt soon after Christmas, which we spent tranquilly on board.

'There is, needless to say, a representative of the Prudential (P. W. Deacon of Canonbury) in the ship, in the guise of an A.B. He introduced himself to me on the occasion of receiving a Christmas package and letter from the Directors, Manager and Principal Officers of the Company. When the mail-bags come on board they are emptied out on deck. While the Master-at-Arms was sorting out the lot in question, Deacon's hawk-like vision detected two similar packages with the Prudential label on them, one addressed to him and the other to me. You may be sure that the contents and the thoughtfulness which prompted their dispatch were fully appreciated on board the *Proserpine*.

'The social life on board is quite good. There is plenty of humour in the ward-room. The mess comprises some exceptionally agreeable and witty officers, and fortunately no unamiable individuals. That is not to say that no one ever has a liver. Among my shipmates are cats, canaries, chameleons, several bullocks (temporarily), and two white rats, the black dog, and the walrus—the two latter, perhaps I'd better explain, are nicknames for an officer and a seaman respectively. The Mikado, the Jew, Champagne Charlie, and Mr. Kipling (myself) are other *noms de guerre*. Our piano, of course, has been ditched along with the book-cases, etc., but if so inclined one can always take a hand at cards between tea and bedtime. In a vessel of this size there is no space for open-air games, such as deck hockey, but by way of compensation life on board is free-and-easy to an extent never obtaining in a big ship.

'Small and lightly armed as she is, the *Proserpine* has had some not altogether unimportant rôles to play. Besides her present job, she has been guard ship, patrolled the North Sea, the English Channel, the Bay of Biscay and Gibraltar Straits, done a great deal of reconnaissance work, and eaten up no end of coal—and coaling is no end of a top-hole beanfeast.

'When the enemy's telegraphic installation, etc., has been destroyed he carries on communication, chiefly at night, by means of lanterns, fires, and so forth. The watch on duty, always on the *qui vive*, was curiously "had" last night. I had clambered up on to the bridge about half-past ten for a breath of fresh air before turning in, and a yarn with the officer of the watch. I found him fatuously chuckling to himself. The ship was close to the shore, and while the searchlight was sweeping the hills a number of little lights had been noticed, appearing, moving, disappearing, reappearing in so mysterious a manner that finally he informed "father". The owner, all the time suspicious that it was really only one of the sub's monkey yarns (as he terms them), proceeded to turn out. After a careful scrutiny of the phenomenon through the bridge telescope, it was at length discovered that these peculiar points of light were simply the reflections of the searchlight in the jackals' eyes, the disappearances, reappearances, etc., were caused as the animals pattered, panic-stricken, backwards and forwards, seeking escape from the incomprehensible light from the sea, and gazing wide-eyed into its white glare. We frequently hear the cries of these creatures as they rage and rave at night over the carcase of some camel, horse, mule, or donkey—war's victims, left to rot on the road-side.

'"What will our next billet be?" is the question again beginning to occupy our attention. But whether it be the will of Allah that I should ever come back or not, never shall I forget this broad, this beautiful bay, its blue waters shimmering in the bright sunshine, its bordering of high purple hills, and over there in the north its bizarre background of great snow-clad mountains.'

Mr. Cooper was destined to return, but not before he had visited Egyptian and Syrian Waters, Sebastopol, Yalta, Novorrosisk, Odessa, Batum, Constanza and Varna. He took part in the arrangements for the evacuation of refugees from Odessa when the Bolshevists entered.

PRU. MAN MEETS PRU. MAN

It will have been noticed in Mr. B. H. Cooper's narrative that he met another Prudential man on board. During the War Prudential men met each other in strange places all over the world, some unfortunately never to meet again.

Mr. D. S. McLeish was in North Russia with the Royal Scots. When the Christmas mail arrived there was a parcel from the 'Prudential'. To his surprise one of his friends received a similar parcel and, after explanations, they discovered they were both Prudential representatives.

Mr. A. Pearse was sent from Training Reserve with a draft to the Egyptian Expeditionary Force and was posted to 1/11th London Regiment. On arrival in Palestine he found the Regiment was commanded by Lieut.-Colonel A. H. Windsor. Thus the Senior Officer and junior Rifleman were both Prudential men.

Mr. A. Strudwick was in Macedonia serving with the King's Royal Rifle Corps under Lieut. Harold Toy.

Mr. G. R. Taylor, who enlisted in the Royal Fusiliers and was later transferred to the Devon Regiment, also met a Prudential colleague through a letter received from the Company. During 1918 he happened to meet a Corporal who told him he had received a letter from his firm intimating an increase in salary and his comment was, 'That's the sort of firm to work for.' He was greatly surprised to learn that Mr. Taylor had received a letter on the same lines. They were both in the Company's service.

Mr. G. Sparrow served in France with the Royal Army Ordnance Corps. Part of the time was spent under the captaincy of Mr. C. F. Warren, now General Manager in Australia.

Mr. J. R. A. Freer of the 9th Yorkshire Regiment (Green Howards) was batman to a young Officer—Lieut. Akers—in Italy. After some time it transpired that Lieut. Akers was a District Office Clerk at Bolton. They stuck together for the rest of the time and Lieut. Akers was with Mr. Freer when the latter was wounded in August, 1918, on the Asiago Plateau. Later Lieut. Akers himself was wounded, losing a leg. They both met again after the War.

Two men who met and, although now retired, still correspond, are Mr. A. Winkley and Mr. R. Thomson. Mr. Winkley enlisted in the Royal Naval Air Service, which was later incorporated with the Royal Flying Corps into the Royal Air Force. He was sent to Lerwick in the Shetland Isles and had some very rough journeys in the North Sea, travelling through mine-fields and handling depth-charges. He also helped build kite-balloon sheds, filled the balloons with gas and assisted in flying them. It was while building sheds that Mr. Winkley met Mr. Thomson, and although on their return to civil life their Prudential duties kept them in different parts of the country their friendship has been maintained.

Mr. R. P. Gubbins was wounded and taken prisoner at Arras in March, 1918. Whilst in hospital at Minden, Westphalia, he met another Prudential man, also in hospital.

Mr. J. E. Davies gave surgical attention to a Chief Office colleague met in a front-line trench at Arras. He was then attached to the 12th London Regiment. Mr. Davies himself was twice wounded; first at Ypres on 8th May, 1915, and later at Polygon Wood on 16th August, 1917, and was eventually discharged on 26th April, 1918, owing to war wounds.

Mr. L. R. Hutchinson was, on one occasion, in an iron lean-to against one of the German pill-boxes at St. Julien early in 1918. He happened to pull his Prudential Diary out of his tunic pocket, whereupon a friend leaned over the bunk above and exclaimed: 'Hello, Hutchy! You in the "Pru." too!'

Mr. J. L. Smith also met a colleague, Mr. L. P. Gay, in the next bed in a hospital at Rouen, in 1916.

Mr. W. M. Gabbatiss met a Prudential man when they were on police guard together in March, 1918.

Mr. V. G. Taylor, when a Captain attached to 59th Divisional Headquarters, was waiting one day for the Field-Cashier. When the Field-Cashier arrived he turned out to be Mr. H. C. Small, also a Prudential man.

Mr. P. W. Burroughs tells the following interesting story in connection with his encounter, which took place in the Retreat of March, 1918: 'After fighting a rearguard action at Havrincourt Wood I was just about to consolidate my Company in a new position when another officer crossed my line with his men. As he passed we recognized each other to be Prudential colleagues, grimly smiled and went on with our respective jobs. On my return to Chief Office I learnt that my colleague had been taken a prisoner of war soon after our strange meeting. The officer was Mr. J. F. Mance who, curiously enough, was one of the first of Chief Office Staff to initiate me into the ways of a Prudential Junior in March, 1909.'

WHAT A BULLET WILL DO

In August, 1915, a letter was received from Mr. A. T. Frew, which gives one or two vivid pictures which are worth recalling.

'The modern bullet makes what I suppose "professional" people would call a "beautiful" wound. The hole is so small it takes some finding in the dark and sometimes the amount of bleeding is negligible. The other day a chap came along our trench, without any bandages and his shoulders bare, walking quite naturally except for his arm, which was tucked in his tunic. I asked him what was the trouble, and he pointed to his chest. Sure enough he had a neat hole drilled right through him from front to back, coming out just under the shoulder-blade. How it missed his lung is a wonder to me. One experience I have had and that is "gas". Last Bank Holiday we caught it, and for about four hours after we had reached comparative safety, I lay stretched out at full length, gasping for breath, coughing and spitting blood. To add to our troubles on this occasion, we got mixed up with a little shrapnel, and had numerous casualties. The only serious one was a friend of mine, who has since died of wounds. He had been walking in the rear with me, but decided that we were lagging too far behind and urged me to get a move on. Being tired I politely declined, so he hurried on to the front of the column and joined up with the officer in charge. They were both hit.

'I see Harold Cooper is among the fallen. Many a scrap we used to have in '04 and '05—and have been pals ever since, poor old chap!'

The final words of his letter are a tribute from the heart to Harold Cecil Cooper, who was killed in action on April 28th, 1915.

THE DESTRUCTION OF THE *KOENIGSBERG*

Here is a first-hand description of the destruction of the *Koenigsberg*, written by Mr. Gilbert Goodman on H.M.S. *Mersey*, 11th July, 1915.

'At last, after three months, we are unmuzzled and I can give you a few details of our movements. We left Devonport on 14th March on H.M.S.P. *Trent*, which had been taken over by the Government for the purpose. The three monitors having been strengthened with enormous baulks of timber inside and out, and all hatches, ports, etc., hermetically sealed, were each taken in tow by two tugs, and in this undignified fashion the Squadron put to sea.

'The original intention, I believe, was for us to proceed to the Danube as soon as the Dardanelles had been forced, but by the time we arrived at Malta it was realized that a good deal of water would have to flow through the Straits before they were in our hands. We arrived at Malta on the last day of March, our speed being six knots, this being the best the ten-knot tugs could do with our battleships in tow, and incidentally just about the normal speed of the said ocean greyhounds under their own steam.

'At Malta I met Keable, who had arrived a week before, having been appointed Assistant Intelligence Officer. After a month's stay it was realized that we should be of no use in the Near East for a long time, so we proceeded in the same manner as before (or rather the *Severn* and *Mersey* did, the *Humber* remaining at Malta). We passed through the Suez Canal (being potted at by snipers on the banks during the night) and the Red Sea, but it was not until we had passed Cape Guardafeu, the north-easterly point of Africa, and turned our faces south that we were definitely told that our destination was East Africa, and our object the destruction of the *Koenigsberg*.

'This cruiser, with a speed of 23½ knots and carrying ten 4·1-inch guns (with a range nearly equal to our 6-inch guns) had been chased by H.M.S. *Chatham*, but escaped up the Rufiji River, in German East Africa, where she lay thirteen miles from the entrance. The general impression in England was, I know, that she was practically destroyed, but as a matter of fact she was very much alive. She had a double crew on board, all her guns were intact, and she was used as a sort of base for their military operations against British East Africa. Moreover, in view of the possibility of her trying to escape, and of the size of the Rufiji Delta and the number of river-mouths, it required a considerable fleet to maintain the blockade. When we arrived we found the *Hyacinth* flying the flag of the Commander-in-Chief of the Cape Station, the *Weymouth*, a modern fast cruiser (badly needed elsewhere), the small cruisers *Pioneer* and *Pyramid*, the armed liners *Laconia* and *Laurentic*, four armed whalers, and our addition consisted of two monitors, a liner, and four tugs. So much for the helpless *Koenigsberg*.

'Our base was Mafia Island, captured last January. It lies about 100 miles south of Zanzibar, and twenty miles from the Rufiji Delta.

'We made our first effort on Tuesday, July 6th. We anchored two miles from the entrance late on the previous night, and got under weigh just before daybreak. When about a mile from the entrance a 12-pounder from the shore opened fire, all the shots falling short. We endeavoured to put it out of action (unsuccessfully), and all the way up the river we carried on a vigorous fight with our 3-pounders and quickfirers against snipers and machine-guns; here of course, we were at great advantage and they got no change out of us.

'At 6.35 a.m. we anchored fore and aft across the stream, so that both ships could bring their forward and after 6-inch guns to bear. We were thus four 6-inch guns against five 4·1-inch, as the " K " could only bring one broadside to bear. They had, of course, " spotting " stations commanding every entrance that could possibly be used, and the chart marked off into numbered squares, so that immediately we anchored they could give our exact position to the " K " and after three or four ranging shots had our range and went into " rapid salvo " firing (very comforting). Our spotting was being done by aeroplane, but our shots were very difficult to observe, and the *Koenigsberg*, of course, did her best to jamb the wireless so that the corrections came through very badly indeed. It is obvious that from this point of view their advantage was enormous, and before we started the officers in the other ships were laying 5 to 1 against our getting out of the river at all. Apart from gun-fire we ran a great risk from mines, and from torpedoes launched from one of the many creeks that feed the main channels. Our anchorage was about five and a half miles from the " K ", and neither ship could see the other owing to the dense growth of mangrove trees on the islands and the banks. By 7 a.m. salvoes of four and five shots were falling all round the *Mersey* (they ignored the *Severn* for some reason or other, probably she was not so visible from the " spotting " station), and at 7.30 a shell burst about two feet from our quarter, and the word came through, " We are holed on the water line "—fortunately this afterwards proved to be incorrect—however, the Captain gave orders to " up anchor " and steam out of range, and it was well he did, for while this operation was going on a shell struck the shield of the foremost gun, killing four men outright and wounding four more, two of whom died shortly after. Half a minute after we left our position, five shells fell on the identical spot, and had we been there then nothing on earth could have saved the ship. As a matter of fact, this is probably the first time in nautical history where ships have deliberately anchored within range of an enemy ship. An hour later we returned to our old position, and from then on until 3.30 the two ships pounded away. We were getting practically no spotting corrections, so we merely increased and decreased the range by instalments, and even in this haphazard way we managed to hit the " K " sufficiently to reduce her gun-fire from five to one gun, and eventually she ceased firing altogether. We retired at 3.30 very dejected, as we had hoped that if we were successful in reaching the anchorage the rest would be fairly plain sailing. The observers in the aeroplane told us afterwards that one of our shells hurled one of the "K's" guns over the side, but apart from that she did not seem to be very seriously injured.

'Our second effort took place on the following Sunday, 11th July. This time it was arranged that the *Severn* should anchor about 8,000 yards from the "K" and fire for twenty minutes; meanwhile, we should remain under weigh bombarding the shore batteries, and after twenty minutes proceed up the river to a range of 6,000 or 7,000 yards, and have a spell. Unfortunately for us the aeroplane was brought down before our turn came, so it was no use our cutting in. Nevertheless, by this time the *Severn* was hitting with practically every salvo, and could therefore carry on without any spotting.

'The following extracts from the log I kept during the action will give you a fair idea of the course of the action:

11.30 a.m.	*Severn* opened fire on banks.
11.35 "	Shore battery opened.
11.41 "	*Mersey* opened on banks.
11.45 "	'M' hit by 12-pounder in Captain's cabin (3 men wounded).
12 noon	Fire lessened considerably.
12.20 p.m.	*Koenigsberg* opened fire with four guns.
12.21 "	*Mersey* opened fire on *Koenigsberg* while under weigh.
12.37½ "	*Severn* made first hit.
12.40 "	'Hit', 12.44 'Hit', 12.44½ 'Hit', and so on. (These are wireless signals from aeroplane.)
12.48 "	'We are hit, send boat for us. All your shots are hitting the "K" forrard.'
12.50 "	Aeroplane came down. Aviators picked up by our motor-boat. Machine destroyed by gun-cotton charge.
1.15 "	Large cloud of smoke observed.
1.35 "	Proceeded up-river past *Severn*.
1.45 "	'K's' masts visible from foretop.
1.50 "	Second aeroplane up. Made signal, 'Carry on firing'.
1.55 "	'2 hits'.
2.10 "	2 hits reported. Possible demolition parties at work on board, or else explosions of magazine. No guns firing at 'K' at the time.
2.12 "	Ditto.
2.16 "	'2 hits' ditto. (This coincided with two explosions seen from foretop.)
2.18½ "	Hit 'K'.
2.28 "	Orders 'Retire. *Koenigsberg* destroyed.'
3.30 "	Opened fire on banks during retirement.
3.57 "	'Cease fire.'

'We left the river to the music of the 12-pounder that had

greeted us on our arrival on Tuesday, but in her four attempts she only got two hits, one of which failed to explode.

'Total casualties: 4 killed, 2 died from wounds, 5 injured.

'*Severn* escaped without a scratch.

'The finest incident to my mind in the whole action was furnished by the aviators who—with their engine stopped, their machine falling rapidly from a height of 3,000 feet, with a choice of crashing into the trees or falling into the water and probably turning turtle—continued to make wireless signals to us so as to assist us till the last possible moment.

'We are now on our way to Zanzibar for a fairly extensive refit, as the poor old monitors are now in a very sorry condition, and I expect it will be a considerable time before I am able to tell you anything very thrilling.'

DESCRIPTIVE LETTERS

In September, 1915, a letter was received from Mr. M. Foulger, who described an ordinary day's routine.

'I will run briefly through an ordinary day's routine (shells, etc., permitting). After the night's work I turn in at 4 a.m., leaving my sergeant on watch, and if all's well sleep till 8 or 9, when I go along the trench and see all the rifles are clean and the trench tidy, etc. By this time my servant has prepared my breakfast, which I very soon eat. After this comes my toilet, which takes me several times as long as when at home, and curiously enough I seem more particular over many things. This takes me to 11 o'clock, when I start getting some of the men to work, and then retire to my dug-out to censor their letters and write my own. At 1 o'clock I go across the road (through a trench) and have lunch with the rest of the Company officers. The afternoon I generally spend in reading or writing, and occasionally indulge in forty winks—tea at 5 p.m., then until 8 I potter about, chatting to the men or looking through the glasses for snipers, etc. At 8 I dine in solitary state, as it doesn't do for me to leave the trench very often, and soon after 9 we start the night work. It sounds a very quiet and peaceful existence, but 'tis far from it, as at all sorts of times they suddenly shell us, and I have to jump up and see all the men get cover.'

A further letter describing Ypres strikes a note of horror—a note which we find now creeping into the letters written. Here is a vivid comment on the shortage of shells.

'We came to the famous Cloth Hall, and I could hear my men exclaim at the terrible scene which confronted them. There was a café a few yards from it, where four months ago I had dinner. Alas! I tried hard to find it, but a few bricks only mark the spot. As we were passing here shells were bursting in another part of the town, and I had a very anxious time getting my men through to the other side, which we were all very thankful to reach, and it was not until we had left that city of the dead well behind us that we halted for a well-deserved rest. After ten minutes we resumed our journey of nine miles back to our billet. Presently we came across a small party of men by the wayside who were lost. I tacked them on to us and on we went. A little farther along we met three men, footsore and weary, who had fallen out from their battalion. One can't but feel sorry for these men, some of them 45 years of age, who after a prolonged stay in the trenches are called upon to march nine miles heavily laden, and if some of the slackers at home could see them it would make them think. All the way home we met and re-met various parties of men and different companies of other regiments resting by the roadside, and, as we passed, mutual friends would call out some jovial remark. Such scenes are, of course, enacted nightly and are very interesting, except when turned into tragedy when a shell lands amongst a party of men. We eventually arrived at our billet at 4.30 a.m., and after seeing my men settled, was soon enjoying tea and eggs.

'On the 11th we returned to the line for another 16 days, and found as usual that our trench could be enfiladed from both ends. However, 'tis bound to be on this "bloody salient", as it is termed.

'The first day passed quietly except for a few gas-shells sent over to annoy us, but the next evening there was a regular bombardment from both sides, and we thought an attack would develop. However, it quietened down again, so methinks it was only what we call "getting the wind up": each side, thinking the other is going to attack, starts shelling to calm their own nerves! This, of course, is always happening with the infantry, and alarms are numerous.

'The next few days we spent most of our time bailing and trying to get rid of the mud, for we have had very heavy downpours, and suffered several bad nights when no work could be done. The ration parties bringing their loads across country had a rough time.

'Although the Huns' trenches were 700 yards distant, they seemed to have eagle eyes and could spot any movement. On our left they occupy a ridge and can see what is going on in our trenches, and no sooner do we start work than shelling starts, so now all our improvements are done at night.

'On the night of the 19th, the Huns bombed an advanced post of ours, and a regular battle followed. We, in the trenches, didn't know what was happening, and were naturally anxious until we had a message saying, " all's well ". They repeated the performance the next night, and we lost several men. It appears that our advanced post collared a hedge which the Germans judged belonged to them, and so tried to turn the usurpers out, but without success.

'As half my platoon were in a support trench, we had to go out digging every night on various jobs, and got through some good work during our stay. Occasionally we had a machine-gun turned on us, and I lost a man two nights in succession, and was lucky not to lose more.

'Very fortunately during the whole of our last stay the wind was in our favour, so except for gas shells the enemy could do little damage to us in that way. Our last day, the 27th, made up in excitement for the quiet of those previous, and we were very glad when we were relieved that night. At 10 a.m. they started shelling us with huge ones, and until 12 o'clock we had a very nervy time. The first one fell 100 yards short, and I laughingly made a remark about a bad shot, not knowing what was in store. The second one burst a few yards from me, covering us with debris, and we were just wondering what had happened when the next one burst right in the trench, killing two men standing a couple of yards from me, and blowing several yards of the trench to bits. The men were terribly mutilated and were a shocking sight. The next few landed in our support trench and half demolished it, but luckily my men had evacuated it, so no one was hit. They then plastered the firing line again, and owing to our being enfiladed, if one dropped short, it simply meant that it fell in the other end of the trench, which was just as bad. This battery was firing straight down our trench, and we all seemed to have miraculous escapes. Five officers, myself included, were standing by our mess when one struck the ground a few feet away. We all thought we had gone to glory, but, lo and behold ! it failed to burst, and we were much indebted to several other " duds ", which would have wrought fearful havoc among us. Another man was in his " dug-out " when a shell came right through it and into the next, bursting a yard away, and he escaped with a shaking. You may ask, " What of our own artillery ? " As soon as the Germans started we 'phoned through and asked for retaliation. Alas ! The guns were silent, but later sent over a few " paper-bags " as my men call them, meaning small shells, which in comparison to the ones the enemy were sending over were ridiculous. It does seem hard on the men in the trenches, especially as I believe they shelled us in retaliation for our heavy sniping of the night before in our endeavour to gain superiority of rifle-fire.

'It is at such times as these that one notices the difference between the men, some of whom are terrified, whilst others wait for the next one with a smile on their face, which after all is the best way, as one can only trust in Providence. I am of course just as frightened, but do my level best not to let my men see it, and at times it is no easy task.

'On our way home we crossed the Yser, and in the moonlight it looked just perfect for a midnight dip. However, a shell-hole near by reminded us that it was unwise to dally, so pushed on and eventually reached our billets at 3 a.m. The next morning at breakfast they gave us an unpleasant shock by starting to shell us. Although we were some seven miles behind the firing line, they put two "duds" in the garden of our billet and several more very close. Luckily no one was hit, but I think it was very inconsiderate of them to spoil our hard-earned rest! The next day was peaceful, but on Friday we had orders to "stand to", ready to move at 20 minutes' notice (this was the result of the latest German frightfulness, liquid fire). We waited in readiness, and at 5 a.m. on Saturday we had orders to move at once, and within a few minutes the company was fully equipped for the fray, and off we marched, all thinking we were in for a show and were at last "going over the top". We marched several miles and manned some reserve trenches and waited for two days expecting any moment to receive orders to go forward. On Sunday night the Huns made another attack and the shelling was very heavy. Everyone was waiting in suspense and as each messenger on a motor-cycle came tearing along, we (the officers) waited almost breathless whilst the Colonel read the messages. But no, we still stayed there, and very soon after things quietened down again. We remained there till last night, when we suddenly received orders to move back to billets, and weren't sorry, although in one way we should have liked the excitement of an attack, but they are far too costly really to be desired. On our way we passed little groups of men who had been victims—or rather those who had escaped—of the liquid fire outrage, and a terrible sight they were, covered in dust and mud, a frightened expression on their faces. We arrived back here at 2 a.m. this morning, and enjoyed tea, etc., and listened to music from an excellent gramophone which we now possess. It is a great treat to hear any sort of music, and we turn it on at all meals, and in fact nearly all day.'

'It is a great treat to hear any sort of music.' A man could write that in the midst of horror. Alas, that so many of those brave

D

hearts were stilled. Maurice Foulger was killed in the attack on Hooge very shortly after writing that letter. Leading his men gallantly and approaching the second line of the German trenches, he was killed by a machine-gun bullet.

'GOD HAVE PITY ON US AS A NATION IF WE FAIL TO TOE THE LINE'

Here is an extract from the diary of Mr. L. W. Lewis, written on April 18th, 1915.

'Ever since our arrival here we have realized that our Brigade has been in the hottest quarter of the line. Whereas trench life is described by the men as a quiet waiting life, not altogether pleasant but quite easily borne as long as there is little fighting, they tell a different tale up here.

'No sooner have they taken over than they find it a continual danger zone. Fighting is incessant. Artillery fire is quite common, and casualties are a matter of course. Things have been very fierce just lately, however, and I am tired of the sound of the guns. They strike a sort of dull, low, mourning note which is inexpressibly sad, and when it keeps on all day and all night it is more than a joke.

'The wounded have been going through the town all day, and it is good there are such suitable places to which to bring them in the town to be dressed. This I fear is all over now. Although the town is commanded on three sides by the Germans, and they are very close to it, until a few days ago they had not shelled it. Our theory was that they were hoping to take it undamaged. But for some unknown reason the day before yesterday they started shelling, sending over more than 300 big shells. You can try to imagine the scene, but will get no idea of the reality of it. Here were people who for months had been living under the noses of the German guns practically undisturbed, encouraged to return to or remain in the town because of the prospects of trade with our troops. Then one fair morning death comes hurtling through the air. These are some of the scenes I saw. In the square a family, comprising a man and his wife, the woman with a baby in her arms, and a toddler holding her skirts and four other children, the eldest of whom could not have been more than twelve years old. Their "home" was contained in a big pillow-slip. That was all they had been able to take away. Their house was in ruins, and they were wearing the clothes they had put on when the bombardment began. Never in all my life have I seen such helplessness as was expressed in the man's face. This, after nearly 2,000 years of Christianity! The nearest town of safety was at least eight miles away.

'If the people in England only knew one ten-thousandth part of what is going on out here there would be no need for the Government to use its voice and its power to coerce people to do their bit. God have pity on us as a nation if we fail to toe the line, and wipe out the stigma and stain of German Kultur as depicted by the smoking and stinking ruins of Belgium. Words fail you as you look on such scenes, and a lump rises in your throat. If you weren't strenuously busy at such a time, you would break down and cry. Three times have I felt the lust of fighting get hold of me: when I saw the wrecked civil hospital shelled when situated in an undefended town, the gassed men brought in from the Canadians, and the city after its bombardment.'

TWO BRAVE GERMANS

In a letter home Mr. H. G. Clifton gave a graphic picture of the capture of a German aeroplane.

'The German Aviatik monoplane swooped down to within about 300 feet above us. Thinking he was going to drop bombs on our balloon we had our rifles ready. However, he didn't, but effected a safe landing in the next field. We all rushed to the scene (cooks and all, so there was no breakfast that morning!). As we approached, one of the German officers turned a machine-gun on us to keep us at bay, and bullets whizzed around us. A company of King's Royal Rifles opened fire on the other German officer who, climbing out of the machine, was in the act of swinging the propeller to start up the engine again, when he fell riddled with bullets. The other officer was eventually killed! It shows how determined they were to the last.'

THE WHOLE STAFF ENCOURAGED TO ENLIST

On the 28th October, 1915, the following notice was issued to the Chief Office Staff by the Directors.

Re The King's Appeal

'On the occasion of the King's Appeal to his people, the Directors once again desire to express their admiration of the patriotic spirit animating the Staff which has led so large a proportion of those of military age to join the Colours since the outbreak of War.

'More than seventy per cent of our clerical staff eligible for Service have already enrolled themselves and the Directors observe with gratification that a large proportion are serving as commissioned Officers, showing that these members of their Staff had either trained in times of Peace or had subsequently spared no effort in becoming qualified, and in any case, that they were willing to accept such responsibilities as they were considered fit to discharge.

'The Directors, in view of the King's Appeal, wish it to be known that it is their intention to continue the encouragement they have afforded to men who have already joined the Forces and to extend the like consideration to all who now see their way to respond to the Nation's call.

'They will not seek to make any reservation in order to retain the services of any members of the Staff excepting to ask that in a few individual cases the call to Service may be temporarily deferred in order to satisfy urgent requirements of the work.

'The Directors are confident that the pride they have expressed in "Prudential" patriotism is fully shared by the Staff; they anticipate that the men still available will offer themselves readily and willingly for the Country's need, and they unhesitatingly rely on a continuance of the self-sacrificing efforts of those not eligible for Service to carry on successfully the business of the Company under the increasingly difficult conditions which must be anticipated, and which will require the most determined efforts to overcome.

'The wish is expressed that the members of the Staff electing to volunteer should do so under the scheme proposed by Lord Derby.'

THREE GOVERNMENT APPOINTMENTS

At the end of 1915, three appointments were made by the Government which were of interest to the Company.

Mr. Joseph Burn was appointed by the Chancellor of the Exchequer to a seat on the Committee to consider and report on the subject of a scheme for making investment in War Loans more attrac-

The City of London V.A.D.

Contingent of 1st and 3rd City of London (Prudential) V.A.D'S.
Lord Mayor's Procession 1915

tive to the working classes, and on the best method of popularizing the scheme.

The then Chairman of the Company, Mr. T. C. Dewey, joined a special Committee appointed to consider the possibilities of economy in war expenditure. The general opinion was that there was considerable scope for the work of such a committee, and the 'man in the street', who believed that the War Office was hopelessly extravagant, and who clamoured for the appointment of business men to assist and advise the Government, was well satisfied with the choice that had been made.

A further honour came our way as a New Year's gift. The Government having appointed representative bankers and members of the Stock Exchange to advise them in dealing with American Securities, sought a business manager to carry out the work, and again it was to the Prudential they looked for the expert assistance they required. The Secretary, Mr. G. E. May, was asked to undertake the onerous duties, and he took quarters temporarily at the National Debt Office.

Mr. Joseph Burn is now Sir Joseph Burn, K.B.E., the General Manager of the Company, Mr. T. C. Dewey later became Sir Thomas Charles Dewey, Baronet, and President of the Company, and Mr. G. E. May is now Lord May.

LOOS

Here is a first-hand description of the Battle of Loos written by Mr. J. H. B. Rich from a hospital at Le Havre.

'The night of the 24th September found us quietly getting into the new trenches and cursing the trench garrison already there for being in the way. The morning was chilly with a deadly drizzle, but at 6.32 15 secs. I took "B" Company out behind a cloud of gas without being able to see more than twenty yards in front, and every landmark by which I hoped to keep direction was out of sight. Immediately the gas started the Boche artillery fairly went mad, and shelled our lines to prevent us getting out, and in between the lines in case we had got out—in fact everywhere and anywhere. But during all this the men lay very low, and as soon as time was up they were out and lying down in line as if on a field day. They were splendid, and on getting the signal they went forward at a jog trot, which rapidly became a walk owing to the stifling effect of what gas had been left behind by the wind. Very soon the German trench came in sight, and the wire, which had been well cut by our artillery, offered but a slight obstacle. Our men were soon on the Huns' parapet. Sheer funk had caused them to get off their fire-steps, and the consequence was that they did not see our men until they were right on them, when the chances were all in our favour, as they could hardly hold a rifle for panic (that is, a good number of them).

'The second line was just a replica of the first, and when we had taken this, our duty was to consolidate it for our use, that is, build a parapet and fire-steps facing the Boche. By this time the 19th London and 20th London caught us up (they were our supports) and went right through for the third line, a thousand yards farther off, and on the other side of Loos village. They got there just in time to kill a few who had not already done a scoot, and in obedience to orders proceeded to consolidate that trench (it was the duty of our Brigade to make a defensive flank on the right). After this, parties of the three battalions proceeded to clear the houses in Loos of Germans who were hiding in cellars, and who had in many cases been asleep when we were already in the town. There we lost many men who were shot by objectionable persons sniping from houses, and who afterwards tried to surrender. . . . The next three days and nights were filled with bombing contests and German counter-attacks which never fully developed owing to the volume of fire brought on them, and their losses must have been very severe. The battalion that held the German front line opposite us was the 22nd Silesian, and their published losses were 15 killed, 42 wounded, 879 missing. Not bad, eh! Our losses were 282 out of 620, about 45 per cent.

'Now the extraordinary thing is, that although during our advance they shelled us like mad and I could see shells going off all over the place, I do not remember hearing a single noise the whole time. In fact the entire performance seems to have been entirely automatic on my part. So peculiar was my state of mind, that although it rained all day I did not notice it, and it was not until next morning that I seemed to come out of a dream and start living again.

'It is remarkable what endurance one has, for from the night of the 23rd no one slept until after mid-day on the 26th, and yet with the aid of the rum ration which came up it did not seem an undue strain. In fact it is far less exhausting to attack than to sit tight in trenches during a severe bombardment.'

Mr. Rich's account of Loos is the fullest we have in our possession, but there were many other Prudential men who took part in this battle.

Mr. A. Follington enlisted on 10th August, 1915, in the R.A.M.C., joining a unit which was under orders for France, and he landed in France 17 days after enlisting. They had no equipment and were in the Battle of Loos without gas-masks, their personal belongings being rolled in a blanket and tied on their backs with rope.

Mr. S. Fleming was wounded in this battle. More fortunate, however, was Mr. G. Howard who, although posted as 'Killed in action', was very much alive and had the privilege of removing the cross from his own grave at Vermelles in October, 1915.

We have also traced the following, still alive to-day, who were at Loos in 1915.

A. R. Allport	F. Izod	C. H. D. Pratt
G. H. Davies	W. Lifford	C. S. Quevillart
G. E. Daviss	H. B. P. Owen	P. M. Stephens
H. J. N. Debenham	C. C. Pickering	F. M. Wakely

THE IBIS RIFLE CLUB TELESCOPE

On 29th July, 1915, Mr. Godfrey Yearsley, writing from 149th Battery, Royal Field Artillery, 146th Brigade, 28th Division, British Expeditionary Force, France, says, 'Do you think the Ibis Rifle Club would lend my battery the large spotting telescope if it is not being used? I know it would be immensely valuable to us and would probably be the means of showing up the movements of German troops in the two towns which our O.P. overlooks. Our battery lost their best glass at Mons.' The telescope referred to was duly sent from Chief Office and on 22nd August, Mr. Yearsley wrote: 'We have been using it this morning from the O.P., and already the glass can claim two scalps. A party of Boches were seen outside a ruined farm about 800 yards behind their fire-trenches, and were apparently having breakfast. Needless to say it did not take us long to locate the spot on the map, obtain the angle from reference line, calculate angle of sight and range, etc., and send this over the 'phone to the battery.'

Later, from an address given as 'The Balkans', Mr. Yearsley gave some further adventures of the telescope.

'The telescope is still safe and sound and doing good work. It has been in some funny places with me. Was in use during the Loos–

Hulluch push, and a few days later when we made the attack on the Hohenzollern Redoubt. On this occasion I was F.O.O. to Brigade and consequently the glass and myself went " across " with the infantry and got into the famous Redoubt. (I have a Prussian helmet as a memento).

'I ought to explain that the telescope was not taken down to the trenches for observation of fire, because at close quarters the field is too small. We used the glass in this case to read morse and semaphore messages, which were being sent from R.A. battle headquarters some distance in the rear. So you see the old glass gets a " rough house " at times.'

A MODERN BATTLEFIELD

About this time Mr. H. Agate gave a graphic picture in a letter of the horror of the battlefield.

'A modern battlefield after the fight is something just too terrible! In this case in many parts the trenches were not recognizable as trenches at all. One might imagine there had been a huge earthquake, causing great holes and piling the earth in high mounds, both holes and mounds containing " cannon fodder ".

'I spent a fearfully gruesome night. Some of us had to go out and form a screen while the wounded were collected. It was very dark and one could scarce avoid treading on the wounded, and often found oneself standing on a dead body! There was the possibility of finding a party of Boches in hiding, so we had to go very quietly, peering and listening. We had some " crumps " disturbingly close. When you hear a shell coming you get as close to Mother Earth as you can. If it is very close you get a flash between the eyes, both ear-drums seem split, and your first thought is, " I am not hit ". These " crumps " will throw stuff up in the air two or three hundred feet and fling up trees just as if they were matchsticks. The cries of the wounded were most distressing. Some had gone mad and were screaming, others despairingly crying out for stretcher-bearers. Many had lain there for twenty-four hours, and knew that if they were not brought in before daybreak would have to spend another day out.

'There is no romance in war now. Even the rifle has given way to the bomb, and the whole thing is cold-blooded murder.'

THE DEATH OF A HERO—DUNCAN HARRY BEDBROOK

Here, perhaps, is one of the finest letters in this book. It tells vividly of the death of a soldier. There are probably hundreds of Prudential men whose names have no mention in this book to whom a tribute such as this should be paid. But in this Bedbrook was fortunate. First he was a brave and courteous English soldier and secondly he had a friend with the literary ability to pay a worthy tribute to him. Hylton Cleaver was then on the Staff of the Company. He left to earn his living by his pen and has since become well known as a novelist and short-story writer.

'In case you have not yet heard, I am writing to tell you that dear old Bedbrook has made the great sacrifice. He was killed in the Push on Monday morning, July 31st, with the Captain of his company and five other men. We have lost so heavily in paying the price of victory that you will understand how a man has to have some very exceptional traits to be honestly and individually missed. One misses one's pals in bulk—four-fifths of a company killed or maimed. But which one of all does one miss most?

'I want you to know, and tell them at home, that when Bedbrook was killed I saw four strong men—four of the oldest "boys", four who had been through Hell unmoved, seen death without fear, and killed their Boche without demur—break down and cry like children; because it was Bedbrook.

'This is the only man, with one exception, that I am writing home about, out of perhaps sixty of whom I should like to tell, and I say without exaggeration that this is because no man in the Battalion was more loved and admired, because no man fulfilled his duty and so perfectly adapted himself to the greatest job in his life as "Bedder", and because no man has been more terribly missed. He died without disfigurement or ugliness at the conclusion of the worst experience he or I had had. He was killed as we were being relieved. We had stood up under a terrible bombardment and driven back two counter-attacks, and through it all "Bedder" was just himself—cheery, brave, and a perfect leader. There was no man who did not feel braver for being beside him. The last order that I remember, given when our last machine-gun had been blown to bits, and the team laid out, and they told him with anxious eyes, brought from him the words—"Never mind, boys; No. 1 will stand to their guns to the last." We did. And when in the morning relief came up, and " Bedder " turned at last to go, he was killed with his finished job behind him.

'I was " Bedder's " pal, and especially of late, when old mutual pals were going by degrees. I had been constantly with him, sharing a funk-hole or a drink of tea or supper at a cottage during rest time. You know and you will understand how his disposition helped a man, and, when there is this much to face and every other friend has gone too, his loss seems irreparable to me.

'He loved his men and his men loved him. He was to one and all out here, to rough and polished men alike, simply " one of the whitest men that ever lived ". He shared all their discomfort, scorning the ease his rank might otherwise have brought him. He had refused the rank of Sergeant-Major because he would not leave his men. At least two men refused commissions because they wanted to stay with him. He had not missed a day in the trenches. He understood each man's character in No. 1 Platoon, and treated each man as a pal, yet never had to speak an order twice. A sergeant's job out here is the hardest job, and " Bedder " made it look easy

'He died in the arms of one of the oldest men, without consciousness and without pain, and he died a very gallant gentleman. He has gone, in the words of a writer, to lead his own dear men up the steep slopes of sacrifice; and I want you to let them know at home, that, without decoration or striking rank, he did more in the war than any man I know to help in the great by helping in the smaller ways, and by keeping to the wheel the shoulder of many men who would have fallen from exhaustion or given up because they were over forty, if any other man had been their leader. But he was " Bedder ". All that was best in him came out in this war, and he will not be forgotten.'

ENTERTAINMENTS TO WOUNDED SOLDIERS

On December 18th, 1915, the first of a series of Saturday afternoon entertainments to wounded soldiers was given in the Hall at Chief Office. Soldiers were collected from various hospitals in London by members of the Red Cross detachments, the number being usually about a hundred. Many first-class artists gave their services and tea was provided after the entertainment. These social afternoons continued throughout the War and were welcomed by the hospital authorities. Some armless, some legless, and some blind, the men displayed an amazing cheerfulness and threw themselves into the spirit of the afternoon with zest.

The Chairman, one of the Directors or the Manager of the Company was always present to receive the guests.

A report of the Christmas, 1916, entertainment describes some of the guests going back to their hospital on a specially chartered tram. Why they went on a tram is not clear but we are told that the soldiers sang lustily ' Back home in Tennessee ' and ' There's a long long trail a-winding ' while the driver beat time with his bell and the conductress pirouetted on the footboard. The report concluded with : ' Lord Macaulay observes in one of his Essays, that the feelings and opinions which pervade the whole Dramatic Literature of a generation are the feelings and opinions of which the men of that generation generally partook. We are not sure that future historians will turn to the pages of the *Ibis Magazine* to discover national feelings at Christmas, 1916, but at least we can say that such a gathering as this does reflect the spirit of the country.'

These entertainments continued until March, 1919, and nearly 3,000 soldiers attended them.

CHRISTMAS, 1915, GREETINGS

As a Christmas, 1915, greeting the following letters were sent by the Company to the men serving with the Colours. The first letter was addressed to those engaged in active Naval or Military service (approaching 2,600 in number) ; the second letter was sent to those who were interned in a neutral country or were prisoners of war ; and the third was directed to 119 men and 129 ladies employed under the sign of the Red Cross at home, and one lady in Malta. The first two letters were accompanied by the welcome gift of a box of chocolates, a card expressive of good wishes, and a copy of the circular letter to the Staff which is quoted on page 44. Well over a ton of chocolate was despatched.

Christmas, 1915.

DEAR ——,

A year has passed since I wrote to those of our Staff engaged on Active Service, assuring them of the deep regard for their welfare which is universally felt by the Directors and by all their Prudential colleagues.

The year has brought us much sorrow and anxiety—sorrow for noble lives gallantly offered and laid down in defence of freedom and in the service of King and country; anxiety for those who have been and are confronted with the manifold dangers which our Naval and Military operations invo ve.

The year has not passed without affording ample evidence of unreadiness on the part of the nation to undertake hostilities upon any considerable scale, and the strain imposed upon our political and industrial systems has at times been almost greater than they could bear.

On the other hand, the unexpected and unparalleled difficulties we have had to face have been met with sustained and glorious heroism on the part of the Services, which has brought added splendour to their imperishable records, and civilians of all ranks are learning to be content with no effort short of that which the most skilful and effective organization can produce. It may, I think, be said that we—men and women—are beginning to apply all our energies whole-heartedly to win the War.

We of the Prudential have been animated by a strong desire to associate ourselves with, and—if it may be—to strengthen and hearten our colleagues who have joined the Colours. Every one of us has been glad, whenever possible, to 'do his bit' by contributing some extra effort to make up for the absence of those on Active Service.

The spirit in which the Company has discharged its responsibilities in relation to the War must fill every one of its representatives with gratification and pride; its attitude to its policy-holders and its Staff alike has satisfied all that fervent patriotism could desire, and any service it has been possible to render to the State has been readily undertaken and fulfilled.

In this connection you will be interested in the terms of a Memorandum to the Staff—copy enclosed—authorized by the Board on the occasion of the King's Appeal to his people in relation to Lord Derby's Recruiting Scheme.

It has always been the desire of those responsible for the direction of the policy of the Company that their relations with the Staff should represent something more than a contract entered into for commercial purposes, and we have been glad and happy to make provision so that our men have been able to leave us at the call of a higher duty without apprehension for the maintenance and comfort of those for whose welfare they are responsible.

We look forward to the day when the scattered members of our Staff will once more be re-united with us in carrying forward the peaceful banner of the Company—a day which seems more distant sometimes than at others, but one which is very surely, it may be rapidly, approaching.

We are glad to hear from all sources of information that there is no pessimism at the Front, and you will believe me when I say that it is practically unknown amongst Prudential men ; it is bred in our bones that difficulties exist only that they may be overcome, and the tradition is an admirable one for the commercial as well as for the tented field.

Even though the way seem long, it will be trod gallantly and untiringly by Prudential men, and Peace shall come to stay with us, with our children and with our children's children, when the military domination of the Hun has been completely and finally destroyed.

The gift of chocolate herewith forwarded is accompanied by our heartiest good wishes for Christmas and the New Year.

Always yours sincerely,
A. C. Thompson,
General Manager.

Christmas, 1915.

Dear ——,

Once again I write to assure you of the interest in your welfare which is felt by the Directors and by all your colleagues in the service of the Company.

We deplore the mischance which separated you from your comrades in arms, and look forward to the time when you will happily return to assist in promoting the peaceful progress of the Company.

In the meantime, if we can do anything to supply your need or to mitigate your anxiety in any respect, we will, on hearing from you, gladly seek to accomplish whatever may be possible in either direction.

It must often, I fear, be a weary time for you ; but your release is surely, it may be rapidly, approaching ; and I trust while the New Year is still young the change which you doubtless ardently desire may be brought about.

The box of chocolate herewith forwarded is accompanied by our best wishes for your welfare.

Always yours sincerely,
A. C. Thompson,
General Manager.

Christmas, 1915.

DEAR ——,

The Directors and Principal Officers of the Company desire to express to you their high appreciation of the excellent work which has been accomplished by those Voluntary Aid Detachments of the Red Cross Society which are composed of members of the Prudential Staff.

There is nothing, I think, which has more touched the hearts of all connections of the Company during the War than the thought of these men and women, eager to devote themselves and to make any sacrifice in order to bring such comfort as may be possible to those who suffer in the cause of Justice and Empire.

For more than a year, every train bringing our wounded heroes into London was met by the Prudential Detachments, who attended, as required by the War Office, at any hour, day or night, and were entrusted with the care and safe transport of these wounded men from the arrival of the train until they were taken charge of at the various hospitals in the metropolis.

They are still taking an active and leading part in this admirable work, though other detachments are now to some extent sharing the privilege which, for so long a period, our men held practically as a monopoly.

It remains only to be said that our men have not chosen Red Cross work in preference to the discharge of the common duty of offering themselves for Active Service. A considerable number are already on Active Service; and all others, without exception, of military age have attested under Lord Derby's Scheme.

There has been a keen desire on the part of the Women's Detachments to render public service in any way and to any degree which was possible, and in a considerable number of cases individual members of our detachments have been released wholly or at intervals from official work for hospital duty.

The competition amongst our members to take part in this work of succour has at times been almost embarrassing, but the strain has been greatly relieved by the readiness with which their colleagues have always been willing to undertake additional office duty.

On behalf of the Directors, the Principal Officers, and all the Prudential Staff, I thank you most heartily for all you have contributed, or been willing to contribute, to the welfare of the nation in the present crisis.

Yours faithfully,
A. C. THOMPSON.
General Manager.

1916: THE SOMME AND AFTER

THE 1ST AND 3RD CITY OF LONDON (PRUDENTIAL) VOLUNTARY AID DETACHMENTS

In an early chapter of this book we described the British Red Cross Society's Scheme of Voluntary Aid Detachments which was started in 1910 and we left the story at the outbreak of the War. We now continue the history from that date to the end of 1916.

On August 31st, 1914, an urgent call was received from the War Office. Stretcher-bearers paraded at Waterloo Station and assisted in carrying wounded to King Edward VII's Hospital for Officers in Grosvenor Crescent. During the following months our members were called on frequently, but they were able to do all that the War Office asked of them. Their work was chiefly to transport wounded soldiers from Waterloo and Charing Cross Stations to the various London hospitals. By the end of September 1,253 casualties had been dealt with, and by the end of November this number had increased to nearly 8,000.

The Management gave permission for telephonic communication to be installed direct with the Chief Transport Officer, and arrangements were made for a squad of men to sleep at Chief Office to deal with emergency calls. Early in September a motor omnibus and a private car were placed at the disposal of our detachments. These enabled patients to be more comfortably and more speedily conveyed to the hospitals.

At the end of October a call was made by the British Red Cross Society for men to join a detachment for service abroad. The following members were selected for duty: Messrs. P. W. Burroughs, G. G. Crowe, L. C. Colebrook, W. G. Elcombe, W. S. Gregory, H. L. Mortimore, A. Reeve, C. S. Stockbridge and C. B. Yardley. The detachment left London on November 10th for a base hospital at Calais.

Throughout 1915 our detachments conveyed wounded to the

hospitals. By the end of the year well over 60,000 casualties had been handled. Pressure on their services was especially great during the early autumn, when they assisted in the transfer of thousands of colonial casualties during the Dardanelles Campaign.

On 23rd March, 1916, H.M. King George V conducted an inspection of members of the London Ambulance Column in the gardens of Buckingham Palace. Stretcher-bearers, comprising a total muster of 350 officers and men, 120 of whom were members of the Prudential Detachments, paraded under the leadership of Commandant W. F. Symons at the Horse Guards Parade, whence they proceeded to Buckingham Palace. Prior to the King's inspection of the ranks, Commandants W. F. Symons and F. V. Simmons were presented to His Majesty by Major-General Sir Francis Lloyd, K.C.B., C.V.O., D.S.O.

As a result of a fund inaugurated by and generously contributed to by members of the Company's Field Staff, it was possible to present two motor ambulances to the British Red Cross Society. The presentation was made on Tuesday, 23rd May, by the General Manager, Mr. A. C. Thompson. The Ceremony took place in the quadrangle at Chief Office and was attended by Sir Thomas Dewey, members of the Management and a large number of the Chief Office Staff. The Field Staff was represented by three of the Company's Inspectors, Messrs. Howarth, Lindley and Rimmer, several Superintendents and Mr. Ross of Edinburgh, to whom the inauguration of the scheme was attributed.

The Hon. Arthur Stanley, Chairman of the British Red Cross Society, attended to receive the ambulances and to express the Society's thanks and appreciation. They were subsequently loaned to the London Ambulance Column. The two ambulances together cost £900 and a balance of £150 was handed to the Red Cross Society as a contribution towards their maintenance.

By November 14th, 1916, the number of casualties transferred to hospitals by the Prudential V.A.D.s had amounted to nearly 140,000 This figure included a large number of wounded German prisoners.

FOR CONSPICUOUS SERVICE

In the July, 1916, issue of the *Ibis Magazine* appeared the following :

" It is with great pleasure that we place on record the fact that His Majesty the King has recently conferred a well-earned honour on our colleague Mr. A. H. Windsor.[1] The official notice is as follows: "To be Companion of the Most Distinguished Order of St. Michael and St. George, Major (Temporary Lieut.-Colonel) A. H. Windsor, 11th Battn. (County of London) The London Regiment (Finsbury Rifles)." '

Lieut.-Colonel Windsor was an old volunteer, and had served in the South African War. He afterwards took a commission in the Finsbury Rifles, and at the outbreak of the war he was a Captain in that regiment. The Finsbury Rifles were ordered to Gallipoli. Captain, shortly to be Major Windsor, soon showed his military ability and was given command of his own battalion.

In 1916 Lieut.-Colonel Windsor was in Egypt conducting desert defences and operations against the Senussi, and from 1917 to 1919 in Palestine and Syria, taking part in the various engagements in which his Division (54th East Anglian) participated.

GIBRALTAR IN JULY, 1916

Mr. H. E. Egleton describes Gibraltar:

'. . . The Rock is a really wonderful place; the upper part is in the hands of the military, but officers in uniform are allowed to wander all over it. There are innumerable walks that can be taken to different parts of the summit without covering much old ground. There are grand views from near the top; several towns in Spain are visible, also Ceuta on the African Coast. Near Ceuta the Spanish and Moors are always fighting. If we happen to get rather close in to this coast the Moors usually take a few pot-shots at us.

'I am picking up a little Spanish; it is much easier than French or German, as there are fewer "exceptions to the rule"; also most words are pronounced as spelt. A knowledge of Italian would help one greatly; a knowledge of French is also useful. There are some clever people stowed away here. A few days back I met an old lady who spoke Greek, Italian, Spanish, English, Hebrew, Arabic, French and German. She was perfectly familiar with the history of all periods and countries, and was quite a politician. To-day an old chap applied to me for a job as steward or cook; he, also, could speak several languages.

[1] Appointed Assistant-Manager, December, 1931.

'House rent is very high here and averages nearly £1 per week for a furnished room. As a rule the rooms are very tiny, but I am glad to say that mine are large, with the exception of the kitchen. Most houses have a tank underneath in which the rainwater is collected. There is no fresh water laid on, but brackish water is supplied for sanitary purposes. I live just behind the Royal Artillery Headquarters, so that I am able to get a soldier orderly to bring up fresh water each day, as we have no tank.

'Football is *the* game here, and the Navy last week defeated the Army and won the Governor's Cup. Grass will not grow here, so games are played on the bare earth. Tennis is very popular and there are quite a number of courts. The Hunt is popular and has frequent meets in Spain.'

THE FIRST BATTLE OF THE SOMME, JULY 1ST–NOVEMBER 18TH, 1916

This battle, which lasted for four and a half months, was one of the fiercest battles of the War. Tanks were used for the first time on the 15th September.[1] They were not, however, the overwhelming success they were expected to be, and it was not until the Battle of Cambrai, 20th November–13th December, 1917, that they were used with really decisive results.

Mr. F. Wharhirst writes:

'This was the first occasion on which tanks were used. It was considered of such importance that there was a rehearsal behind the lines. Hopes were high that the end of the war seemed near. Such hopes were soon dispelled when it was seen how easily one direct hit from an enemy gun put a tank out of action.'

On the 16th September Mr. Wharhirst sustained a fractured tibia and fibula, being subsequently graded C.3 and attached to an Assistant Director of Medical Services.

Mr. D. M. Cowan also witnessed the opening of the attack by the tanks at 6.30 a.m. He was one of a party from Battalion Advanced Headquarters detailed to carry ammunition to the front-line troops about 10 a.m. on the same day. Only seven of the party of twenty returned. Two days later he was caught in a shell-fire barrage and

[1] Mr. J. L. Cogdale was engaged on experimental work on the first tank constructed.

2ND/5TH EAST KENT REGIMENT ('THE BUFFS')

H. L. Coleman, F. G. Sibley, A. N. Pellett, G. C. Cocking, H. F. N. Coles, B. Hardie, P. F. G. Sayer, F. C. Capon, H. M. Binsted, G. H. Mallett, G. Walbancke, F. T. Chitty

had the butt of his rifle smashed whilst carrying it slung butt upwards on his right shoulder because of the rain.

Mr. R. Greenwood, who went over the top on the 1st July, was one out of only forty-seven survivors of his Battalion.

Mr. W. E. Hegarty witnessed an Armistice to bring in our wounded from No Man's Land during the afternoon of the opening day of the battle at Gommecourt (1st July). He says: 'As our own guns at the rear continued firing the Germans (Bavarians) gave us ten minutes to get clear. We remained half an hour.'

Mr. B. T. Sayer arrived on the Somme on 1st July and his Division —the 23rd—captured Fricourt and Contalmaison.

Others who took part in this battle whom we have been able to trace were:

J. Allison	B. Gardner	S. M. Ruse
H. Andrews	L. P. Gay	J. Shuttleworth
G. R. Aucutt	J. Griffin	H. Street
J. D. Ballantyne	W. Lifford	J. M. Stewart
J. A. Bissett	J. McBay	R. G. Sweet
J. Blagg	F. Morcom	A. Symons
H. S. Coles	R. Perriam	E. H. Thomas
A. M. Dowell	C. C. Pickering	N. Todd
J. C. Edmonds	F. W. Poupard	F. M. Wakely
W. Emblen	R. H. Priscott	F. Warr
E. Firth	F. Rasor	E. Whittaker
J. Forde	F. Raybould	
A. F. Gale	J. A. D. Ribbons	

The following who also took part in the battle were wounded:

C. V. Alder	T. Lye	H. Stillwell
H. G. Hartnoll	W. F. Rice	R. V. Taylor
W. H. Jessop	D. Smith	

AN INTERESTING PHOTOGRAPH

We publish here a photograph of a group of Chief Office men in the 2nd/5th East Kent Regiment (' The Buffs ') taken in September, 1916. It is interesting to see what their fortunes were to be.

H. L. Coleman served throughout the War and became a 2nd Lieutenant in the R.A.S.C. F. J. Sibley was killed. A. N. Pellett finished as a Lieutenant in the R.A.S.C. and was not demobilized until August, 1919. In April, 1918, he had a lucky escape, a shell bursting immediately under his horse. G. C. Cocking was discharged in 1917 owing to wounds. His left elbow was shattered by shrapnel as he went over the top. H. F. N. Coles finished as 2nd Lieutenant, Labour Corps, in charge of a Labour Detachment. B. Hardie was killed.

P. F. G. Sayer went into the line on the Somme front. In May, 1917, he was the last man left out of about a dozen holding a shell-hole and became a prisoner of war. He returned to England in December, 1918. F. C. Capon spent most of his service in the Ypres Salient and became a Lieutenant. He was wounded on 21st March, 1918, at La Fere, being one of a mere handful left of his Battalion, the remainder being killed or captured. H. M. Binsted was gazetted in June, 1917, 2nd Lieutenant, East Surrey Regiment. He was taken prisoner of war at the Battle of Cambrai, November, 1917, and spent a year at Saarbrucken. G. H. Mallett served fourteen months in France and was wounded on three occasions—once seriously. He was awarded the Military Medal and Bar and was twice mentioned in dispatches. R. Walbancke was captured on 3rd May, 1917, near Arras, and not released until 29th December, 1918. His experiences are included in the chapter on Prisoners of War. F. T. Chitty was gazetted Lieutenant in November, 1918. He took part in the Battle of Cambrai.

A MODEST BUT IMPORTANT JOB

Writing in September, 1916, Mr. C. F. Frost says:

'. . . Broadly speaking, our work is to inspect everywhere, and then stamp out and remedy any kind of insanitary conditions that we find or which may be brought to our notice. This involves work of most varied nature, including disinfecting, latrine building, incinerator building, road sweeping, burying, draining, and countless other things. All this, perhaps, is not very much in itself, although extremely useful, but you will realize that it may not be such a soft thing when carried out under war conditions, and frequently under shell-fire or in gas.

'Last Sunday I was sent to help finish a disinfecting job at a place we only took a few days before. It involved two days' work after I arrived, and we slept about two and a half miles away in a dug-out in the abandoned trenches. Even there we were shelled.

'As for the job; a château (Contalmaison) which had been badly knocked about by the bombardment, contained two cellars, the room of which was needed. These cellars were full of debris, and a very unpleasant odour, which was found to be dead Germans! And it was a five days' job simply to clear the place.

'We were saved the trouble of digging holes to bury rubbish in, as these were amply supplied by shell-holes all round; but it was quite exciting enough to carry rubbish to the holes with shells literally bursting all round you, and my eyes were streaming with water from the effect of the "tear" shells. I was only some half a dozen yards away when the already ruined tower received another blow, and some more of it fell down.

'You may read in the papers that "such and such a village or wood" has been captured, etc.; nothing could be more of a travesty than to call these places by such names now; they are absolutely unrecognizable as such, there is positively *nothing* left that is repairable. Even where we are billeted at present, in a fairly large town (Albert) behind the original line, I have not seen a single whole house.'

Mr. Frost joined the R.A.M.C. in 1915. Whilst in France he and four other Prudential men had the experience of being officially lost by the War Office for some weeks through being sent to the wrong base camp. Later he was in the 5th Army retreat. He became Lieutenant in the R.F.A. and was wounded in September, 1918.

'WE WENT OVER THE TOP'

A vivid story is furnished in a private letter of Lieutenant C. H. Cole dated September, 1916, from somewhere in France. He writes as follows:

'... Why I am alive to-day I really do not know. We went over the top on Saturday afternoon. I am the only officer of the company left, and one of only two left when the battalion came back. On Friday night I did a bombing stunt with the Battalion Bombing Officer. We took the trench, which was only 4 ft. deep. All night we dug ourselves in, but bad luck was our lot; the morning was very misty and the Germans crept up and bombed us out. Well, after that I returned to my platoon, and in the afternoon took them over. It was awful, shells and bullets all round and the ground covered with dead men. I wasn't a bit excited. I thought I was going to die and so determined to die doing my bit. I walked along cheering up the men, telling them to keep in a line. When we got to within about thirty yards of the German trench I looked round for my boys. I was the *only one* standing! So I jumped into a shell-hole ! Having got my breath back I climbed up the side to do some sniping. I saw a big Boche chucking bombs for all he was worth, so I laid a bead on him very carefully and waited till he was right up—then bang ! One Boche less ! Then I think a bomb must have knocked me unconscious, because when I woke up it was just getting dark. When I got near the trench we started from I thought I would make sure we were still in it. I saw some hats, but they looked like Gerboys' spikes, so I waited for a " Vérey Light ", which the Germans kindly supplied in about ten minutes. I then saw to my great relief that they were our boys, so I immediately stood up straight and yelled, " Don't shoot ! " When I got in the trench the M.G. said, " Well, sir, good job you stood up, I was just thinking of dropping you." We were shelled all night, and in the morning they got the exact range of our trench and killed a lot. One of the Captains went off his head, and what with him and all the wounded I had *some* time. Then nobody else would go back for help, so I went and took back the Captain. When I got to H.Q. I fainted with shell shock, so they put me in a dug-out and I had a rest for the day.'

On October 3rd, Lieut. Cole was killed in action. His Commanding Officer wrote of him, ' He did his duty at all times, never failing in the smallest degree. He was cheerful under any conditions and his courage in times of danger was an example.'

HIGH WOOD, SEPTEMBER, 1916

The following letter has historical interest, but it was not written by a Prudential man. It was, however, written by the son of a Prudential man, Mr. C. Redway, to his father, and we feel justified in including it. It describes vividly the advance at High Wood.

' We left on Thursday, September 14th, 1916, at noon, in marching order, without packs and great coats, 48 hours' rations, 220 rounds of ammunition, a bottle of water (which, by the way, lasted me three days), a bomb in each side-pocket, rolled waterproof sheet, and a shovel which we carried on our backs.

' We had no sooner arrived at our attacking position on the right edge of High Wood than we had our first casualty, one of A Company's officers being killed outright by a shell. The position of this trench was about 400 yards to the far edge of the wood. By aerial observation it was assumed that the enemy were entrenched only 200 yards away behind a slight ridge.

'At 6 a.m., a small rum ration was passed round. A few minutes later, my platoon officer, Mr. Kelly, in giving us last advice by walking along the parapet, fell on top of me with a bullet through the hand. Realizing that the correct time was everything, as we were going to advance with a screen of shell-fire moving slowly in front of us, I snatched his arm, and at the advertised time, 6.20, gave my Platoon Sergeant, Sergeant Taylor (who was decorated for Loos), the tip. No. 1 Platoon went over, the other platoons followed at distances of 50 yards.

'We advanced to within about 50 yards of their trenches amid a storm of rifle and machine-gun bullets. There seemed to be a momentary lull; the Huns were coolly standing up, head and shoulders above their parapet, picking us off. It was a matter of do or die; and, knowing by past experience the German courage, I started a terrific yell, which was promptly taken up by everyone. First one strafer, then another, lost their miserable courage, and soon the whole lot dropped their rifles and ran like mad. I shall never forget that moment; we got them on the run, and the old gag of "Merci, Komrade", was uttered too late.

'Another hundred yards brought us to a diagonal support trench, which was also used as a communication trench. A few more were disposed of with the bayonet. My Sergeant was hit, so I took control. According to orders, our objective was a fourth line, about in line with the far edge of the wood, which by this time was nearly captured by another London unit; but on arrival this trench was *non est.* I blew my whistle and halted. The ground was one mass of enormous shell-holes; by placing three men in each and connecting up, we had quite a fine line.

'. . . Our area was now being taped by the enemy, and for five days we simply sat tight and "did nuffink", like Brer Rabbit. During this period all kinds of troops visited us until it got uncomfortably crowded; at one time I had about forty under my control and in no communication with Headquarters or officers. The line was lengthened on both flanks by the same method, but casualties were not nice; we had no end of dead and dying.

'I cannot give details, but it was one long nightmare. Water was scarce and cigarettes soon gave out. I was buried twice, and knocked silly for some hours by concussion.

'We will now skip to the relief: how we shook hands and when on the road in the rear I believe we had a fiendish war dance. The day was spent cooking. We had hot drinks, and attempted to sleep in some fine old German dug-outs a few miles back—but our happiness wasn't long lived, for a runner brought in orders to turn out and take rations up to an advanced post. We started at 7 p.m., and by compass got to this destination at 6 a.m., having walked round in a circle three or four times.

'. . . Every officer in my company except one has "gone under" and he is now in hospital with a nervous breakdown. All Sergeants and the Sergeant-Major wounded ; so yer 'umble has the honour of bringing A Company of the Shiny Seventh out of action alone.'

Amongst Prudential men who took part in this engagement was Mr. G. R. Aucutt of the Royal Field Artillery.

Mr. J. C. Edmonds, who was also in this area at the same time, tells of an amusing occurrence :

'Our Waggon Lines were in Death Valley and I and another Sergeant were detailed to proceed with a working party to an advanced point very near High Wood, in order that our 18-pounder guns might be brought into action by bridging the trenches.

'As the enemy were continually firing salvos which burst very near us, it was necessary for me to shout to the men to take cover.

'At that moment a party of prisoners was being escorted down the line, and apparently mistook the shouting for an order to shoot them, for they raised their hands and shouted "Kamerad".

'This situation caused much amusement as none of us was armed.'

A PRUDENTIAL Y.M.C.A. HUT

Much good work was done by the Y.M.C.A. for the welfare of men at the Front and in military camps at home. Men serving with the Colours gladly availed themselves of the many privileges afforded by the Y.M.C.A. at the sign of the Red Triangle. The Directors of the Company, in recognition of this service, agreed to defray the cost of a Prudential Y.M.C.A. Hut to meet the needs of the troops in the town and district of Chelmsford. The building stood on a large plot of ground, the property of the Company, opposite the railway station. The term 'Hut' conveys a very inadequate idea of the accommodation provided, which comprised a large entertainment hall, seating 400 soldiers ; a canteen, with room for two billiard tables ; a separate 'Quiet Room' for reading and writing ;

a kitchen and storeroom; some bedrooms for the staff and several bathrooms.

The opening ceremony took place on December 19th, 1916, when about 400 guests were present at the invitation of the Mayor and Mayoress. It had been intended that Sir Thomas Dewey should formally present the building to the Association and that Mrs. W. E. Horne, who was a warm supporter and active helper in their work at Guildford, should declare the building open. Unfortunately Mrs. Horne was ill at the time and Sir Thomas was not well enough to be present.

Sir William Lancaster read the speech which Sir Thomas Dewey would have delivered had he been present. Mrs. Schooling declared the building open, and the Bishop of Chelmsford read the dedicatory prayers.

The ceremony was followed by a speech of acceptance on behalf of the Central Council of the Y.M.C.A. by Colonel Sir Sturmy Cave, K.C.B.; and Colonel Muirhead, Royal Scots, acknowledged the gift on behalf of H.M. Forces.

Mr. A. K. Yapp, afterwards Sir Arthur Yapp, the General Secretary of the Y.M.C.A., expressed the thanks of the whole Y.M.C.A. movement to the Company, and said he did not believe there was any investment they had made of which they would be more proud than the money they had put into the building.

A musical programme followed at which at least five hundred men were present. During this programme Mr. A. K. Yapp gave an interesting account of his visit to France and related many incidents in connection with the work in camp and in the trenches.

THE GENERAL MANAGER

In October, 1916, came the news that the second son of the General Manager, Mr. A. C. Thompson, had been killed. Mr. and Mrs. Thompson thus lost both their sons.

Also came the news that W. S. Halford was killed in action on 15th September. Halford was a book-lover and a poet and died a good and dauntless soldier. On his last night he wrote: 'It is curious that a pacific person like myself should be chosen for these affairs.' In a letter to a friend written ten days before his death he said :

'Out here the people bear their almost unbearable burdens with a magnificent stolidity. When the history of this War is written the glory of France will shine through it like an ineffable dawn, and in that glory the women of France will have played an imperishable part. We burned Joan of Arc in the market-place of Rouen, but her soul glows in the hearts of these women, many widowed, and more childless, aged and wrinkled, many past admiration, often dirty, who in the house, the farm, the fields, in all weathers so superbly "carry on".'

Halford was one of many of his type who made the supreme sacrifice. We set his words in print as we think he would have liked them to be remembered.

CHRISTMAS GREETINGS, 1916

When Christmas came the Directors and Principal Officers of the Company again sent letters, Christmas cards and chocolates to their colleagues serving in the Naval or Military forces, and also to those interned or in the hands of the enemy as prisoners of war.

Parcels were dispatched as follows :

To those in England	4,398
To those in France	1,522
To those in Eastern countries	472
Sailors	61
Prisoners of war	20
	6,473

The total weight of these, when packed, amounted to approximately five tons.

The following are copies of two of the letters sent.

Christmas, 1916.

DEAR ——,

You have been much in the thoughts of all your Prudential friends—Directors, Officers, and other colleagues—during your enforced absence from our dear country or from those other scenes of activity in which, with your comrades, you would be desirous of participating.

Be very sure that our interest in your welfare has not diminished, and that we shall at any time be glad to do anything in our power to help you, and to assist, if possible, those who may be wearying for your return.

We shall continue, as in the past, to provide for the comfort of dependants and to 'keep the home-fires burning till the boys come home'. We accept without reserve the assurance given to us in many charming letters that the recollection of the sacrifices willingly and gladly made by the Company in this connection will be gratefully preserved and cherished ; and we look forward with pleasurable anticipation to the time when you will once more be associated with us in civilian works and life.

We much hope that the barriers which separate us may soon be broken down, so that you may be restored to your relatives and friends, in which latter class all representatives of the Company will desire to be included.

We hope you will enjoy the chocolate herewith forwarded, and regard it as a token of our good wishes for your continued well-being.

Ever yours sincerely,
A. C. Thompson.
General Manager.

Christmas, 1916.

Dear ——,

Those of our colleagues who are members of Voluntary Aid Detachments of the Red Cross Society have had a strenuous time throughout the war ; and it is desired by the Directors and Officers, representing the members and all the Staff of the Company, to express the highest appreciation of your devotion to the country, and also of your loyalty to the Company, for many of you, whenever it has been possible, have successfully discharged the dual duty during the past ; and we are very confident that all, men and women alike, have done their very best.

It should not be forgotten that your frequent or occasional release for the performance of this glorious National Service has thrown upon your official colleagues an amount of work which, added to their own duties, has taxed their energies to the utmost ; and I am sure you will wish to join in appreciative recognition of their patriotism and loyalty, which has rendered possible the accomplishment of both duties.

You have earned the gratitude of those who, whether temporarily or permanently broken in the war, have looked to you, and not in vain, for such tender sympathy and care as you have been able to render, and you have richly merited the respectful admiration of all your Prudential colleagues.

Ever yours sincerely,
A. C. Thompson.
General Manager.

1917: A GRIM YEAR

'THE YEAR DAWNS OMINOUS AND MENACING'

JANUARY, 1917, found the country facing the future steadfastly—even grimly. Let us read what a Prudential man writing at the beginning of the year has to say.

'The New Year dawns ominous and menacing amid the lurid clouds of war; great events and momentous issues wait us in the fateful months to come. The enemy's suggestions for the discussions of terms of Peace may indicate the beginning of the end, or may be but the prelude to a renewal of spitefulness and frightfulness. Who can say? The curtain rises and reveals the same scene and the same chief actors: the stage is set for battle, the war-drum throbs, the bugle is sounding, and the world awaits with breathless interest the further development of the Great Drama. It is the last act that is now to be played, and how will it end? What alarums and excursions, what tragic happenings, what deeds of glory shall we witness before the curtain falls? Or shall we be surprised by a sudden transformation scene with triumphal processions, flying banners, joyful peals, sunshine, music, and laughter? Who dare foretell?'

Alas for the flying banners and joyful peals! Our colleague was to see even more tragedy and sorrow than he had ever dreamed of before the year was out.

MISSING—MAY, 1917

The news that husbands and sons were reported missing was causing agony to many thousands of women in the country at this time. We single out one story which we have secured as representative of many. This story is told by Mrs. Lilian M. Keen, a Prudential wife who lives today and treasures the memory of her husband's sacrifice.

Albert George Keen enlisted in May, 1916, joining the 'Banker's Battalion', the 2/5th East Kent Regiment (The Buffs). During his military training he spent some time working on a farm in Sussex; but he was eventually drafted into another battalion of the same regiment, and went to France on December 24th, 1916. For some weeks his Company was engaged in road-making, and during this period he wrote many cheerful and humorous letters to his relatives and friends. Early in May these letters ceased, and presently letters and parcels which had been sent to him were returned.

No notification concerning him had been received, and for six weeks his wife and friends could obtain no news. At the end of that time it was learned from the Regimental Records Office that he was reported to have been wounded on May 3rd, near Arras, a few days after he had reached the front line. Since no further news arrived, it was assumed that the wound was slight and that he had returned to his unit. But no letters came and at length it was obvious that he was 'Missing'.

His wife made every possible effort to discover what had happened, and after long inquiry the British Red Cross found a sergeant of another company of the same battalion who believed that he could give information. He knew a man of the same name who had been taken prisoner before his eyes, during a German surprise attack. Months passed, and this was the only evidence available; but attempts were constantly made to secure further proof. The Swiss Red Cross took up the search, and a prominent Member of Parliament, afterwards a Cabinet Minister, prevailed upon the German Red Cross to make an investigation. At length a letter was received from a Red Cross official in Berlin, stating that no English soldier of this name could be found in any hospital or prisoner's camp in Germany.

After a long time of suspense, Mrs. Keen was able to get in touch with a man in Birmingham who had been in the 'Banker's Battalion' and had known her husband well. This man had lost a leg and had been invalided home. He told how, in a shell-hole, he had accidentally met another member of the old battalion, who said that 'Keeno', as they called him, had been 'knocked out'. He had no more to tell, but he supplied the information that his informant was a young bank clerk whose home was in Warrington. A little later, it was learned that this young man had returned to Warrington, maimed for life, and Mrs. Keen asked a relative to find him.

When found, he told a remarkable story, which there is no reason to doubt. He and Albert Keen went, in the same company, to the front line in the neighbourhood of Arras. One morning they were with a detachment which had managed to capture an advanced German bombing trench. This they held through the day against heavy bombardment, in the course of which Keen had been wounded in the side. They had made him as comfortable as possible, and he lay there smoking a little and occasionally talking. When night fell, stretcher-bearers came out to convey the wounded to the British lines, and Keen was carried out of the trench.

During the night, the bank clerk and another man were sent back to the lines to get water. The German guns were still busy, and in seeking for cover these two became separated. Creeping alone through the darkness, the bank clerk stumbled over a man lying on the ground, who tried to speak to him. To his surprise, he recognized Albert Keen, who at first seemed dazed, but presently was able to explain that he had been wounded a second time, in the head, as he was being carried on the stretcher. He remembered being hit, but could recall nothing more until he found himself lying on the ground alone. Apparently the stretcher-bearers, thinking him killed, had left him there, and had returned to help other wounded.

The bank clerk, a slightly built youth, was physically incapable of carrying him, but he promised that he would try to procure a stretcher. On reaching the lines he did all that was possible to obtain help. No stretcher-bearers were available. Time was passing, and his duty was to get water. Greatly distressed, he was compelled to abandon his search for help.

Next day the British made a successful push and the bank clerk then implored the stretcher-bearers who were going out to look for wounded, to make a special search for Keen. As nearly as he could, he described the spot where he had found him. They returned saying that they had searched, but could find no trace of him. No trace was ever found. But in those dreadful fields, ploughed and churned by the German gunfire, many a search was unavailing.

He was a lover of life, light of heart and blessed with a sense of humour. He was intensely interested in his work, and also a serious student. He was a wide reader, fond of the theatre and music. He sang well. He was a cricketer and an oarsman. He enlisted because, as he said, his conscience would not allow him to see fathers of families going into the army while he was privileged to remain at home. And he went, smilingly, counting the cost, but willing that it should be paid.

MISSING—BUT RETURNED

Friends and relations of other Prudential men also experienced the same agony of mind as Mrs. Keen. But there were 'Missing' stories which had happy endings. Here are a few.

Mr. R. H. Copeman was officially reported as having died of dysentery on 17th May, 1916. He still has the official records of his decease together with numerous letters of sympathy.

Mr. R. S. Stanfield took part in several engagements, the last being outside Merville on the Armentieres Sector in April, 1918, when he was taken prisoner. As he was severely shell-shocked and physically exhausted he was sent to Quedlinburg (Hartz) Hospital, Germany, where he remained until repatriated on 1st January, 1919. Meanwhile, in England, his wife had received a letter from the Earl of Lucan notifying her of his death in action.

Luckier still was Mr. S. S. Redgrove who, although captured on 21st March, 1918, was able to write to his wife on 29th March telling her of his safety. As he had been posted 'Missing, believed dead' it is easy to imagine what joy his post card brought her. By a happy coincidence it reached her on her birthday.

Mr. A. Challis was reported missing, but actually he was made a prisoner. Mr. R. Leyshon was also reported missing—killed.

Reported killed in action Mr. E. T. Shilling some time later went to a dinner at Portsmouth Guildhall and found his name on the list of killed and heard the 'Last Post' sounded for him.

Not only does the story of Mr. R. Harrison have a happy ending but it was, in itself, amusing in the fact that the letter received by his wife stating he was reported missing and killed about 23rd March, 1918, arrived in January, 1920, ten months after he had arrived home.

BEREAVEMENT

There lies a tragedy behind these lines which appeared in the May, 1917, issue of the *Ibis Magazine*. The writer was Mr. James

Dimmock who was too old for active service but whose son, 2nd Lieutenant J. B. Dimmock, was serving in France.

THANKSGIVING

How can I pray Thee, Lord, to save my son,
When week by week the countless thousands fall?
When horrors upon horrors us appal,
How can I say with faith, 'Thy Will be done?'
If Thou art God of Love omnipotent,
Yet dost not hold the hosts of hell in sway—
How can I go on bended knees to pray,
When bitter tears and prayers seem impotent?
But I can thank Thee, Lord, for my dear son—
The bright young life that knows not shame nor fear—
To whom the call of duty sounded clear,
And forthwith to the fight went bravely on.
And I can pray—if sorrow or if joy—
I may be worthy of my gallant boy.

Before the next issue of the Magazine appeared 2nd Lieutenant J. B. Dimmock had died of wounds. Later in the year the bereaved father wrote these lines :

BEREAVEMENT

'O my son Absalom, my son, my son Absalom ! Would God I had died for thee, O Absalom, my son, my son ! '

A memory of laughing eyes of blue,
Of tiny clinging hands, and twinkling feet
That never seemed to tire, and lips so sweet
Whence kisses came as fragrant as the dew.
Of pleasant happy games in childhood's hours,
The schoolboy's eager zest for work or play,
And youth's ambitions, growing day by day,
Towards the burgeoning of manhood's powers.
Now he has gone—gone in his glad young prime—
And I am left, whose task is nearly done.
The Vision Splendid's closed, and heights sublime
Of good endeavour will not here be won,
Nor may we see the fruit of his springtime.
Would I had died for thee, my son, my son !

MESSINES

The Battle of Messines was one of the outstanding victories of the Great War. On June 7th, 1917, at precisely 3.10 a.m., nineteen mines containing 600 tons of explosives were fired and General Plumer's Second Army captured the Ridge. 8,000 yards of gallery had been tunnelled before the Ridge was destroyed and on the centre Corps front alone—roughly 3 miles—were massed 718 guns and howitzers, 192 trench mortars and 198 machine-guns.

Mr. E. H. Lever, who was serving with the Second Army at the time, describes this hour as one of his most vivid recollections.

'. . . Zero hour (3.10 a.m.) of the attack on the Messines Ridge when the nineteen or so mines which had been so laboriously prepared under the enemies' lines exploded and, apart from direct damage, shook the whole countryside for miles around! I have especial reason for remembering that morning as, almost simultaneously with the opening of fire by our own batteries, an 8-inch enemy shell penetrated our dug-out. Fortunately I was unhurt.'

Here is an experience of Mr. P. C. Hughes, then a Lieutenant of the 23rd London Regiment.

Mr. Hughes was mentioned in dispatches for his part in the Battle of Messines, being awarded the Military Cross for distinguished service at a later date.

'Of all the experiences I had during the War, I think the Battle of Messines remains most vividly in my memory.

'During my eight months' stay in the Ypres salient prior to the great battle I had charge of a sniping section which, on many occasions, meant lying between the trenches dressed in brown suits which toned with the Flanders' mud or, if snow was about, white suits. Our faces, too, were appropriately disguised.

'My job in the Battle of Messines was to establish a forward headquarters for my Brigade and afterwards to go forward and ascertain the positions of the front-line battalions and to send back reports. For this I had my snipers augmented by signallers, runners, linesmen, etc.

'Great efforts were made to keep the actual date and hour of the attack secret and we learned from prisoners afterwards that these were quite successful.

'Our Battery Areas seemed to have grown guns every few yards—

large and small—previous to " Z " day—as the day of the attack was known.

'Zero hour had been fixed for 3.10 a.m., June 7th, and by 2.30 a.m. every man was ready in his place and heartened by a good breakfast.

'To one who saw the dull glare of the exploding mines—I must have been within 800 yards of them—and the continuous flashes of our guns, and who heard the rumble of the explosions mingled with the crash of the shells and rattle of machine-guns, this zero hour will always remain a very vivid recollection.

'The ground trembled with these vast subterranean explosions and the debris hurled high into the air and all around us could be seen against the grey dawn of the morning sky.

'We had to wait in the front-line trench whilst the first three waves of infantry went over the top, by which time the Huns had awakened to the fact that they were being attacked and had started plastering our lines with every calibre of shell.

'Our turn came to go over and just before this I had looked over and seen the troops going well and prisoners and wounded coming back.

'An Artillery officer came walking along the parapet and we exchanged words regarding the battle when—" ping " ! A bullet hit him and he fell dead on top of me.

'This surprised me as he had obviously been hit in the back.

'I gently laid him down and stretcher-bearers nearby took charge of him. I then started to climb over when a fusillade of shots whizzed by. This was not so good, and after a Council of War I gave instructions to follow me over with all haste, not all together, but at intervals along the trench.

'It can be imagined we did not hesitate to get over quickly and with a six-foot drop into the old No Man's Land we landed there safely with the exception of two who were shot in the head and killed instantly.

'I should say here that previous to the attack I had, from the study of an aeroplane photograph, selected an enemy machine-gun post for my advance headquarters.

'On we went, being shot at all the time. We could not understand this until arriving at the machine-gun post I had selected, we found it manned by the entire crew of some twenty of the enemy in charge of two officers. Owing to the rapidity of the advance this post had been missed in the main attack and the crew had temporarily gone to earth.

'We finally surrounded them, and they put up their hands. Those who did not come out of the dug-outs we bombed out. The rest we sent back to our lines without escort as I had no men to spare.

'We established our headquarters and I left the signallers and linesmen to connect up with the Brigade whilst my comrades and I went forward to find the front line which was not too comfortable a task as the whole time we were in the open and under observation.

'It was during this reconnaissance that I ran across Captain G. A. Coombe [1] who, with his Company, was holding part of the line.

'The memory of this day will always remain with me, but particularly the memory of the Artillery officer who, I now realize, saved my life.'

Mr. A. Perryman also has a story to tell :

'We were in action under light cover in a canal facing and within 1,000 yards of Hill 60 when it was blown up with Wytschaete Ridge and Messines Ridge. Within an hour there were hundreds of prisoners around us. The explosion was just like an earthquake and put our guns quite three degrees off the line of sight.'

Both Mr. G. W. Stephenson and Mr. H. Andrews were themselves blown up and Mr. F. Raybould, Mr. F. G. Seward, Mr. A. Pike, Mr. J. Elmes and Mr. J. V. Healey were wounded in this battle.

Mr. H. C. Small took part in the artillery bombardment following the blowing up of the Ridge.

After the attack Mr. O. P. Franklin recalls :

'Outstanding in my memory is the carrying of the wounded after the attack at Messines Ridge. I witnessed a stretcher-party of four, together with a wounded man, blown to pieces by a shell 100 yards in front of my own party. We had to traverse the same track for seven hours against the terrific noise of our own guns and the bursting enemy shells. On this occasion we made temporary use of the German prisoners to assist in carrying the wounded of both sides.'

[1] Mr. G. A. Coombe joined up on 14th August, 1914, a private in the 5th Seaforth Highlanders. In November, 1918, he was acting Major, 24th London Regiment. In August, 1917, he was awarded the Military Cross.

Mr. H. S. French gives a vivid picture. This was written in July, 1917:

'... I took part in the recent operations on the Messines Ridge, and worked very hard, day *and* night, for some weeks previously, in preparing for the final blow. It was certainly a great success, but I'm blessed if I can make my horror and disgust for war generally subservient to my pride in fighting for a just cause. You have no idea what a massed bombardment is like—the Germans must have seen the nearest approach to Hades. Then, the battle-field afterwards, with its corpses, wreckage, filth and stench, must, I should think, convince any sane man of the awful horror and sin of war. I read the other day that *one day's* expenditure on the war would rebuild the slums of London. Does it not seem wicked and *very* foolish that wealth and life should be spent in *de*-struction instead of *con*-struction? However, it's a painful duty, and the quicker we get on with it the sooner it will end.'

Mr. French was in Egypt from October, 1915, to April, 1916. He was posted to the 41st Division on Ypres Sector from January, 1917, and took part in the battles of Messines, Tower Hamlets, Gheluvelt and Passchendaele.

THE SOMME IN SEPTEMBER, 1917

Mr. W. J. Redway, who enlisted in the London Rifle Brigade, spent three winters—1915, 1916 and 1917—in and out of the line. He took part in the battles of the Somme, Arras and the Third Battle of Ypres, and was wounded on the Menin Road in August, 1917. In a letter written from a hospital he gives a vivid description of the Somme conditions in September, 1917.

'The Somme battle was now in full swing and on September 8th we detrained at Corbie and marched to a valley of mud, water and desolation—christened by someone with a peculiar sense of humour, "Happy Valley". We endured six weeks of the Somme, with three attacks. The first attack was a feint to attract German artillery from our real attack, which was further to our left. At a signal from our Company Commander we left our trenches and shell-holes in the wood and, in spite of artillery and machine-guns, took the first German line. But soon after we were given the order to retire, which we did under intense shell-fire, suffering casualties. After this nerve-racking attack, having been reinforced by large drafts, we relieved some troops of our Division in front of Combles.

'We survived four days of rain and heavy artillery. I was rather fortunate as regards shelling, being too close to the German barricade to be shelled by " ours " or " theirs ". The disadvantage of this position, however, was that you had to " Stand-to " all night in case of bombing raids. We had a " cushie " time in the end, as the Germans evacuated at two o'clock one morning, owing to the Allies having fairly surrounded Combles on the right and left. As soon as the Huns left us, patrols of our battalion and the French on our right joined up and advanced through Combles. We dug in on the other side, the Germans having left considerable war material, guns and wounded behind. A week later we were sent up to Les Bœufs to relieve the London Scottish. We made an advance here, and captured several prisoners and guns, but retired to our original position during the night. The day following this attack we were relieved by a French Division and left the Somme area for a rest and reorganization. Had a splendid rest of more than a week at Picquigny, in October, which the battalion sorely needed, as even out of the trenches on the Somme you slept in shell-holes or old dug-outs, as there wasn't a house or wall standing for miles on those shell-battered slopes. An idea of the conditions may be gathered from the following story.

'A Middlesex ration party came across a trench which they believed to be the front line held by their men. They shouted out, " Are you the 7th Middlesex ? " The reply was a shower of stick-grenades and rifle-shots. They dropped the rations, except one man, and those who were not too badly hit fled, leaving rations for a Company and three jars of rum in the hands of the Boches.

'We held trenches in the Neuve Chapelle and Laventie Sectors from November until the middle of February, with the usual attacks occurring at intervals—raid patrol-parties, wiring-parties, and the innumerable fatigues always associated with trench warfare. This was quite a pleasant change after the incessant shelling on the Somme. Soon after the Huns commenced their strategical (?) retirement we took over some trenches in front of Arras. They evacuated Beauvais, leaving several contrivances behind, the chief of which was not discovered until a considerable time afterwards. In order to reach our new front line with rations, water, wire, etc., the carrying-parties passed through the village ; the Huns left some wire connections by which their batteries knew when troops passed down the road, so every night parties had to run the gauntlet of shells, which were usually too close to be comfortable. Another Brigade of our Division took part in the opening offensive of Easter Bank Holiday. We relieved them a few days later, after they had pushed the Huns through Neuville Vitasse and a considerable stretch of country beyond. Here we succeeded in bombing the already battered enemy down several long lines of the famous Hindenburg Line, which looked to me as though it had not been quite completed, although there were plenty of thick belts of wire in front of them. Owing to the rain, sleet and cold, the battalion was very much exhausted by the time our relief turned up. Quite a considerable number were frost-bitten. Two weeks later we returned to the trenches which we had established on the eastern side of Wancourt and took part in a successful attack in the neighbourhood of Cavalry Farm, a considerable number of prisoners being brought back. Our next trip found the battalion in front of Monchy le Preux, and although we received a severe shelling, losing several splendid men in a German attack, the casualties were on the whole very slight'.

DEATH OF MR. SCHOOLING'S SON

On 21st June, 1917, the Rev. Cecil Herbert Schooling, the son of Mr. and Mrs. Frederick Schooling, was killed by a shell. As Senior Curate of the Parish Church at Croydon he had worked hard for the good of the parish. In November, 1916, he resigned his curacy and left for the front to take up the duties of Chaplain. Mr. Frederick Schooling was a Director of the Company and Deputy Chairman at the time of his death in 1936.

GERMAN BUSINESS METHODS

An example of the thoroughness of German business methods in 1917 is given in the record of a claim paid by the Company at that time. The policy was on the life of a child who died. The sole surviving parent was a prisoner of war in Germany.

To comply with the requirements of the Friendly Societies' Act, it was necessary that the father's signature should be obtained and a form was accordingly sent to him in order that the money might be paid to a representative in this country. The amount due was under five pounds.

The document reached the father safely, and was duly signed by him in June, and witnessed by a fellow-prisoner of war, and then the German authorities took the matter in hand.

First the Hauptmann and Lager-Kommandant appended a statement, written in German script, to the effect that the signature was in the handwriting of the prisoner ; the General-Major certified to the signature of the Lager-Kommandant and affixed the prison stamp. The document was next sent to Hanover, where the Inspector of War Prisons certified the signature of the General-Major, affixed his seal or stamp, and sent the paper on to Berlin.

The Prussian Minister of War took up the game, but probably having some other important business on hand at the time, the matter was held up for nearly three months. Eventually, however—on 31st October—he duly verified the certificate of the Inspector of Prisons, and affixed the seal of the Königlich Preussiche Kriegminister, and the document was sent to the German Foreign Office where, on the 9th November, the signature, and two more seals or stamps were affixed, and the German Foreign Office verified the signature of the Inspector of Prisons, who verified the signature of the General-Major, who verified the signature of the Kommandant who verified the signature of the prisoner of war.

In the end the paper was sent through a neutral country to our own War Office, who returned it to the Company with a translation of the various certificates. In the meantime, of course, the Company had paid the money.

PRUDENTIAL POLICY HOLDERS

While on the subject of policies we are able to quote two other instances, one in the nature of a coincidence and one which strikes a more tragic note.

Mr. H. Golding served in Belgium, France, Italy and Greece. On arrival at Salonica on the 18th May, 1918, he marched to a very large English camp. '. . . The Officer commanding the camp inspected the new draft and on passing me ordered the Adjutant to take my name. I was instructed to attend the C.O. Orderly Room at 10 a.m. When I did so the officer asked the others to retire, which they did. He then stood up and put out his hand saying, " Pleased to meet you, Golding. How was my mother when you last called upon her? . . ." It appears that the officer's mother was a Prudential policy-holder. The officer knew of this and also that Mr. Golding was the agent who called upon her.

Before joining the service Mr. J. Steer insured a man who lived at Woking. Several months later they served together in the same Battery at Vimy Ridge. After Mr. Steer's discharge he paid the man's widow a death-claim. His former client and comrade in arms had been killed in action at Vimy Ridge, but our colleague did not hear of his death until he came to pay the claim.

CRICKET IN 1917

In 1917 the cricket ground in London belonging to the Company was being used for military purposes. The following conversation is alleged to have been overheard in the Pavilion on the occasion of a match, 'Officers *v.* Men'.

First Officer: (returning, somewhat ruffled, after being caught brilliantly in the long field). 'Who was that caught me?'

Second Officer: 'Brolhook.'

First Officer: 'Brolhook! What's he doing down here? I gave him seven days' C.B. yesterday!'

THE THIRD BATTLE OF YPRES, JULY–NOVEMBER, 1917

On July 31st, 1917, began the Third Battle of Ypres. It is generally known as Passchendaele. It achieved little except loss. A gloomy story in the records of the War relieved only by the inexhaustible powers of endurance shown by the men.

The area around Passchendaele had been reclaimed from marshland by centuries of labour. The battle destroyed the drainage system and the battlefield became a swamp.

Many Prudential men served in the Ypres Salient during some period of the War and took part in various engagements. However, those we have definitely traced who are alive to-day and took part in the Third Battle of Ypres are as follows :

L. G. J. Adams
W. R. Adkins
W. Allan
J. Allison
F. Andrews
F. W. Barber
A. C. Barnett
J. Carpenter
H. B. Chapman
W. H. Chasty
H. W. Coates
A. Coleman
J. Crutchley
C. J. E. Daily
A. M. Dowell
E. G. Fincher
E. Firth
H. Fisher
H. E. Fossett
H. S. French
F. H. Garraway
J. Glen
J. Gore
C. J. Gratton
A. Hadley
R. Hall
W. L. Hall
F. G. Hancock
L. Hanks
F. J. Hawkins
T. R. J. Herbert
G. E. Hunt
W. J. Hunt
W. F. Jackson
W. H. Jessop
E. M. Jones
G. King
A. Lancaster
R. Lannigan
A. S. Lawton
W. Lifford
S. G. Luxton
O. W. Makin
R. H. Marston
S. J. May
H. S. McFarland
A. W. Messum
D. Milnes
W. A. Mitchell
J. R. Munday
J. O'Donnell
W. Oliver
G. Painter
W. G. Parry
R. Perriam
S. M. Poxon
A. R. G. Pudden
J. Raynor
S. S. Redgrove
W. J. Redway
A. G. Renouf
J. Rhodes
J. A. D. Ribbons
S. M. Ruse
W. L. Sadler
H. J. Satchell
A. B. Smith
C. F. Smith
E. Spencer Smith
G. S. A. Smyth
A. V. Steel
R. C. Stevenson
W. A. Tackley
J. Taplin
S. G. Thompson
J. W. Walker
E. G. E. Watts
P. H. E. Wood
W. J. Wykes

This list obviously gives only a small proportion of the Prudential men who lived through this battle.

For these men and all those whose records we have been unable to secure, the memory of Passchendaele is irradicably impressed on their minds.

Mr. E. H. Lever tells us, twenty years after the event, that the most clear recollection that remains with him is the 'indescribable discomfort, muck and filth of the operations in the Ypres salient'.

Mr. C. Eccles recalls how he took ammunition by pack-horse to guns which were up to their axles in mud, passing through Dead Horse Road in which the corpses of men as well as horses were always to be found.

THE BATTLE OF CAMBRAI, NOVEMBER 20TH–DECEMBER 13TH, 1917

'On November 21st the bells of London'—to quote B. H. Liddell Hart—'rang out in joyous acclaim of a triumphant success that seemed a foretaste of victory, perhaps at no distant date. And Ludendorff, back at the German Supreme Command, was hurriedly preparing emergency instructions for a general retreat. Both the bells and Ludendorff were premature—although prophetic—by some nine months.' It was on November 20th, 1917, that 381 tanks, followed by infantry, moved forward to attack on a six-mile front and gained a demoralizing initial success. Bitter and fluctuating fighting followed and ultimately the greater part of the original gains had to be evacuated. But the Battle of Cambrai is usually regarded as the 'curtain raiser' to the drama of the autumn of 1918.

A very incomplete list of names is given—a few of the many Prudential men who took part in this historic battle.

L. G. J. Adams	C. J. Gratton	W. T. Owen
F. Andrews	C. D. Green	E. E. Penny
H. Andrews	F. W. Hales	H. V. Pinkess
H. Ayres	F. W. Holgate	F. G. Seward
E. Barnard	W. H. Humber	J. Shuttleworth
A. C. Barnett	W. F. Jackson	V. H. Skipworth
H. M. Binsted	W. H. Jessop	H. Smith
H. H. Bloxham	E. Johnson	L. H. Stanton
F. T. Chitty	E. W. Joseph	W. Tapper
P. E. Connor	D. J. Lewis	F. M. Wakely
T. J. Demott	P. McDonald	F. J. Ward
A. H. Eales	E. Newham	E. T. Whittaker
E. G. Fincher	B. H. Newton	R. A. Yardley

THE 1ST AND 3RD CITY OF LONDON (PRUDENTIAL) VOLUNTARY AID DETACHMENTS

On August 31st, 1917, the Prudential Detachments completed three years active war service. During this time some 222,100 casualties had passed through their hands. Whilst on duty at Victoria Station a fortnight later, the 14th September, the detachments were inspected by Surgeon-General Sir Francis Trehearne, K.C.M.G., D.D.M.S., who congratulated the V.A.D.s on the splendid work they were doing.

On November 9th, H.R.H. the Duke of Connaught watched contingents of men of the London Ambulance Column unloading a hospital train. He was deeply impressed by all he saw, and in a visit to Sir Arthur Stanley, Chairman of the British Red Cross Society, shortly afterwards, he spoke highly of the efficiency of the column.

About this time a scheme of reorganization was found necessary. Surgeon-General Sir Francis Trehearne assumed the position of Director of the Ambulance Column, London District. Commandant W. F. Symons was appointed Assistant Director of the Bearer Section, and Commandant R. B. Crothers, Assistant Director of the Vehicular Section. Commandants W. F. Symons, F. V. Simmons, F. H. Tallack, S. J. Toms, R. B. Crothers, A. Hastie, Sir William Savory and P. Runciman were given controlling direction of the Ambulance Column, subject to responsibility to General Sir Francis Trehearne through the Assistant Director.

A TANK COMES TO CHIEF OFFICE

On the 5th December, 1917, the City of London enjoyed the interesting spectacle of a war-worn tank, on leave from the Front, visiting the Chief Office of the Company. The object of its visit was to receive at the hands of the Chairman a cheque for £628,800, being the largest individual contribution to War Savings in connection with the financial campaign then being conducted.

Hundreds of people congregated in Holborn to witness the proceedings and Sir Thomas Dewey made a speech from the top of the tank.

Afterwards tanks visited Sheffield, Liverpool, Portsmouth, Cardiff and other towns to receive at the hands of our local representatives the amount of the local investments, and to announce the sums.

INTELLIGENCE WORK BY PARACHUTES

The following account was sent to us by Mr. L. Pickrell. Mr. Pickrell enlisted in August, 1915, as a Wireless Pupil in the Royal Flying Corps. In 1916 he was transferred to the Kite Balloon Section and in 1917 was promoted Corporal and later Sergeant Mechanic. He served in France, Belgium and later in Italy on the Piave and Asiago fronts.

'The method adopted on the Italian front to drop spies behind the enemy lines by means of parachutes was as follows:

'The rear observer's seat of the aeroplane was removed and the floor of the fuselage converted into a trap-door hinged at the front and secured with bolts at the rear. On this trap-door was seated the person to be dropped, his legs dangling through a gap between the rear end of the trap-door and the fuselage. His parachute was also fixed in a special way and flexible steel control wires ran from the bolts to the front cockpit.

'When the 'plane was over the place chosen for dropping the spy, wires were pulled, and down he went. As soon as he reached the ground the man rolled up his parachute and harness and buried it. He carried food, pigeons and arms and further supplies were dropped by small parachutes at pre-determined dates and places.

'The drop was carried out at night, and the parachute was made of black silk and black tape. It was usual to drop a few light bombs to camouflage the operation.'

'SO LONG AS IN THE END WE MAY BEAT THE BOCHE'

A letter describing his experiences in France written at the end of 1917 by Mr. G. J. S. Hubbard concludes:

'. . . It might possibly be of interest to those who for various reasons are not able to take an active part in the war to know that we are not yet "done to a frazzle" (to use an Americanism), and are willing and content to carry on the work so long as in the end we may beat the Boche.'

That was the 1917 spirit.

CHRISTMAS, 1917, GREETINGS FROM THE COMPANY

As in the preceding years, men serving with H.M. Forces were remembered by the Directors and principal officers of the Company, and received a gift of chocolate and a letter from the General Manager. Of the following letters, the first was addressed to sailors and soldiers, and the second to members of the Red Cross detachments.

Christmas, 1917.

DEAR ——,

During the past year the feeling of the vast majority of our people at home and abroad has developed steadily in the direction of increased determination to attain the objects for which we reluctantly entered the War.

Our people, whether on Active or Civilian Service, are more than ever resolved that Europe and the World must now be liberated from the long-endured threat of German aggression which, for more than forty years, has increasingly become the basis of the policy of the German Government—a policy which has been acquiesced in and, in effect, supported by the full concurrence of the German people.

In the furtherance of this resolve it is the privilege of those on Active Service to bear the foremost part; it is a part full of honour, often full of danger; it has been borne with undaunted courage, often with matchless heroism. We can never forget the splendid sacrifices which have been freely offered in order to win Freedom and Liberty which it will be the privilege of our Statesmen, working in concord with those of the Allied Powers, to establish and confirm. We assure you that you are ever in our minds, and that anything we can do for your welfare is, and will be, most gladly undertaken and performed.

It has been our privilege to help our men to serve the country by affording them relief from financial loss, by freeing them, whilst they are on Active Service, from anxiety concerning the material welfare of their dependants, and by assuring them of advantageous re-employment when they are able once more to return to civilian work.

More than this you do not ask from us, less than this we should think unworthy of the Company.

Our newspapers have given much prominence to the activities of individuals who seem to think that their desire to re-establish Peace among the Nations is stronger than that entertained by other people. If Peace could have been maintained in 1914, on honourable terms, we should not have entered the War.

The aggressive policy adopted by Germany cannot be extinguished by talk, or it would not have thriven for more than forty years; it will not be overcome by resolutions of committees, however well-meaning these may be. The best Peace advocates are our men on Active Service, who have made wonderful progress in spite of wellnigh overwhelming difficulties, and who are rapidly nearing their goal.

Our hearts are torn by the universal suffering and desolation, but we look forward with you, as we have done since war was forced upon us in 1914, confident in the justice of our cause and inflexible in our determination that there shall be no 'next time'.

The Directors, Officers, and others of your colleagues join in sending best wishes for your welfare, and pray that God may bless and keep you and, in the near future, bring you back to your people and to the Company, rejoicing in the complete accomplishment of your heavy task.

Believe me,
Ever sincerely yours,
A. C. THOMPSON,
General Manager.

Christmas, 1917.

DEAR ——,

The work of the Prudential Voluntary Aid Detachments of the British Red Cross Society has been carried on during the past year under exceedingly difficult conditions, and it is my privilege to express to you on behalf of the Directors and all connected with the Company, their unstinted admiration of the praiseworthy spirit which has enabled all obstacles to the patriotic and sympathetic discharge of these duties to be overcome.

We know that many of you have sacrificed not only the leisure which ordinarily eases the burden carried by the strenuous worker, but that in response to urgent need, imperative demands have been met only by the postponement and curtailment of those periods of rest necessary to secure a moderate degree of comfort in one's daily life.

You have, indeed, a glorious reward in the gratitude of the gallant men whose needs and interests you have placed before your own, and also in the knowledge that in this time of sore trial you have done all that has been humanly possible for the welfare of our country's cause, not infrequently at grave risk of personal hazard and suffering.

We are aware that the services you have rendered have been actuated by motives amongst which the hope of reward finds no place, but it is due to your official colleagues that some expression of their congratulations and good wishes should be conveyed to you, and it is a real pleasure to tell you of their whole-hearted appreciation of your splendid work.

Always sincerely yours,
A. C. THOMPSON,
General Manager.

1918: ENDURANCE AND VICTORY

COURAGE NOW BETTER THAN HOPE

HERE is the Editorial Note from the *Ibis Magazine* of January, 1918. The writer now refrains from prophecy and will not even express a hope. Determination to win and to face the future bravely, is as strongly marked as ever. Courage is now better than hope—

'Since 1914 we have, at the beginning of each succeeding year, expressed the hope that success to our arms and a satisfactory peace would be secured before the year came to an end. The hopes so frequently expressed have not been realized. In the year 1917 it was always the unexpected that happened, and the position today is so full of complications that none dare attempt to foretell the course of future events. Our confidence in the final issue is unabated, but the disappointments of the past and the inscrutability of the future compel us to forbear prophecy, and whatever hopes we may still cherish shall remain unspoken. We face the future, however, with a determination to meet all the chances of fate with that unfailing courage which is better than hope ; whatever privations or deprivations the coming months may bring shall be cheerfully borne ; in all the vicissitudes of fortune that may await us, we will emulate the valour and fortitude of our brave men at the Front and upon the sea, and as we go forward into the darkness of the year 1918 we " face the darkness undismayed, and greet the unseen with a cheer ".'

THE TRAINING OF AN AIR PILOT

Here is an interesting account of the training of an air pilot written in January, 1918. It gives an outline of the first stages that a newly-commissioned officer in the Royal Flying Corps had to pass through after being posted to a Squadron for elementary flying instruction. The tragedy behind this account is that Norman Kearney, the writer, died on April 27th, 1918, as the result of an accident while flying at Andover. Lieut. Kearney was flying an R.E.8 machine, and had just left the ground when apparently engine trouble developed. The machine stalled when 50 feet from the ground and nose-dived to earth. Death was instantaneous. Although of a somewhat delicate constitution, at the outbreak of war he made several attempts to join the Army, but failed to pass the medical test; he, however, eventually did so, and enlisted in the East Surrey Regiment, rapidly developing into a keen and smart soldier. He saw service in France, was in the first Battle of the Somme, and wounded at Guillemont in September, 1916. Upon his recovery he was granted a commission, and eventually transferred to the Royal Flying Corps, where he made such progress as a pilot that his services were retained in England for purposes of instruction, and it was whilst so engaged that he met with his sad end.

'The Squadron to which I was posted on leaving Oxford,' runs his letter, 'was No. 1 Training Depot Station, whose aerodrome is situated somewhere in Lincolnshire, and all my remarks refer to a procedure adopted there.

'On arrival, the new pupil is allotted to a "flight" for flying instruction and to a squad for ground instruction, i.e. classes on aerial gunnery, bombing, signalling, photography and artillery observation. The instruction is so arranged that while one-half of the pupils are receiving ground instruction the other half are at the aerodrome for flying instruction. The programme is changed weekly, so that every squad has early morning flying (that is from dawn) during alternate weeks, this being as a rule the best time of the day for flying instruction.

'Ground instruction is just as important as flying, for no matter how efficient a pilot may be with his machine, he will be quite useless overseas unless he understands thoroughly the methods of everyday use.

'Aerial gunnery comes first in importance, and much time is devoted to mastering the Vickers and Lewis machine-guns, control gears and the use of ring-sights and deflection. Firing practices are carried out on the range in order that the pupil may become familiar with, efficient and confident in the use of the two guns.

'Next in importance perhaps is artillery observation. The pupil is here taught all the codes in use at the Front, how to carry out work in co-operation with the artillery, and how to observe and report when on reconnaissance or patrol. He must also be able to read Morse signals on the ground at the rate of at least four words a minute; in wireless signalling a rate of eight words a minute, sending and receiving, is required.

'In bombing instruction pupils are taught the composition of explosives and detonators used in the various types of bomb, the construction and fusing of bombs, the different uses for which certain types of bombs are made, the method of dropping, and the sights used to enable pilots to take aim at the target on the ground.

'There is also instruction in aerial photography.

'The pupil detailed for early morning flying must rise before the dawn and be at the aerodrome in time to make full use of the first daylight while the air is still and unaffected by the rising sun. It may be surprising to the uninitiated how soon the sun affects the air, and renders an otherwise perfect day quite unfit for instruction. The heat of the sun causes air-pockets and upward currents of hot air which throw the aeroplane about in what is, to the pupil, an alarming manner. Before the pupil is taken up, an instructor always goes up to test the air conditions. These having been pronounced fit, the pupil puts on his helmet and climbs into the front seat of a machine which is fitted with dual controls, and off he goes on his first instructional flight.

'He is taken up to 1,000 ft. or so, and then given the machine to control, first learning to fly straight, then to make turns, and finally to land and take the machine off the ground. This of course takes many flights and several hours of instruction in which to get perfect. However, as soon as the pupil shows himself efficient, he is sent up by himself to do exactly as he likes in the air. Before passing out to a higher instructional squadron, he must do four hours flying by himself and make at least fifteen landings, and also let out the aerial of the wireless set five times.

'During my own flying instruction I have had several exciting experiences, including two crashes and many solo flights.

'Generally speaking, the airmen are divided into three classes; (1) the reckless, who are employed on fighting and scouting; (2) the tireless, who are employed on long distance bombing raids and long reconnaissances; (3) the intelligent, who are employed on artillery work and photography.'

INTERCESSION SERVICES

On the mornings of March 18th, 19th, 20th and 21st, 1918, a series of Intercession Services were held in the Hall at Chief Office for the 7,450 of the Staff on Active Service. Two of these were arranged for the men and two for the ladies, each lasting about fifteen minutes. Mr. A. C. Thompson presided at the first two and Sir Thomas Dewey at the latter two. The Bishop of Stepney addressed the ladies at the meeting on the 18th, and the last was addressed by the Bishop of London. Short addresses at the two intervening meetings were given by the Rev. J. Stuart Holden, Vicar of St. Paul's, Portman Square, and the Rev. E. F. E. Wigram, Hon. Indian Secretary of the C.M.S.

THE LUGGAGE SQUAD

One feature of the War was that everybody, whatever might be his or her age or physical defects, tried to do his or her best in some way, be it glorious or humdrum. The work at Chief Office was now being carried on by men who were either over age or had some physical disability which made it impossible for them to be accepted for military service. Most of these men, however, served with the Voluntary Aid Detachments, which meant that they spent a large amount of their time both day and night at the railway station transporting the wounded to hospitals and did their full share of clerical duties at the office as well. But wounded officers had luggage and their luggage had to be looked after. Here is an amusing description of the Red Cross Luggage Squad written by one of our colleagues who was voluntarily doing this work at the time :

' It is your privilege periodically to become one of a luggage squad, and the chastening effect of the work will be for the good of your soul. The first duty of a luggage squad is to find two trucks, and having found them to sit on them until the train arrives. If any wandering porter should attempt to steal them for the use of the civilian population, he must be ordered off. On the arrival of the train the luggage squad trundle their trucks up and down the platform until they find the luggage-van. Having found the van, they unload its contents on to the trucks, and trundle the result to the end of the station, where the various articles are arranged in three straight lines and resemble a rummage sale. There are shilling walking-sticks, old boots, tin helmets, camp-beds, boxes, bags and valises. You are then supplied with a list of hospitals, and you mark everything you can find with a big blue pencil, designating to what part of London the boots and helmets are to be sent. After that you start work in earnest. The proposition presented to you is three long lines of luggage and one motor-van, and the luggage must be packed in the van. One of you gets inside the van to arrange the articles as they are hurled in. (If you are over four feet in height that part of the work should be avoided.) Then two, working together, stagger about the platform grasping valises, trunks, and boxes, studded with hundreds of nails, corners, and splinters. As you reach the van you give the article a mighty swing, and one, two, three—up she goes. Bang! In the meantime your colleague inside is arranging things neatly—pushing and struggling and bumping his head and scratching his hands and wrestling and perspiring until at last every nook and cranny is filled and every box loaded up. The van is full except for about five inches by four. That spot is reserved for you to sit on as van boy. You clamber into your alleged seat and the van slips out of the station *en route* for the garage, where the luggage is to be sorted out. As you watch the road slipping quickly under your feet you hope you won't pitch off, because you feel that, as a member of the Red Cross, it is your duty to assist in a street accident by putting on splints or holding back the crowd. To be the injured man yourself is not part of the programme. On arriving at the garage you empty the van and sort the luggage out for the various hospitals, then load up again for one of them, and start out once more. You do this all day and all night and finish up looking like a sweep.'

THE SPIRIT WHICH WON THE WAR

We have tried, as we said before, to set down in this book the human story of Prudential men in the War. The individual records and stories quoted have been chosen because we thought them typical of most men who served. We again stress that this is not a complete record but a picture. One great difficulty has been the very natural and laudable diffidence of men to say what they really did. A good example of this was provided by Mr. Norman Galloway who, when asked to give details of his War experiences, wrote this simple statement. 'I enlisted on 15th February, 1915, in the London Scottish and served in France for three years without distinction.' Yet unknown to him we have come across a letter written to a friend in 1918 in which he says:

'My battalion recently has been in the thick of the Boche offensive, and only a very few of us are left to tell the tale. I am the only officer left in my Company. Our C.O., Adjutant and all the officers who were in action are all gone with the exception of three —one being myself. You will see by this that we had a pretty rough time, and I am now hoping that leave will start soon. It is now five months since I made my second visit to this country, and it seems like five years. We now have a big draft to make up our strength and they are a sturdy lot of youngsters. Two or three days ago I was going round the front line, which is close to the Boche line, and I noticed a dug-out with a board outside with the words, "Oldham Town Hall", written on it. I said to a man inside, "Where is the Mayor?" and he replied, "Oh, he has gone fishing, sir!" That is an example of the sort of spirit that exists out here, and I might say the spirit that is going to win this war.'

Norman Galloway was right. This was the spirit which won the War and which we believe is still the spirit of the average Englishman.

FLANDERS–1918

Lines written by Mr. E. S. Robertson in April, 1918.

'Oh! Why are you booming, Great Guns out in Flanders,
And turning the stillness of night into Hell?
The darkness is rent both above and around
With the flame of your breath, and the scream of your shell.'

'We devour all we get from the gunners who feed us.
The Gunners! God knows they are paying their toll.
And our breath is destruction, but would you have other?
Your women are safe, and your children are whole.'

'You spit, and you crack, Little Guns out in Flanders;
A laugh in your voice—God! It's bitter to hear.'
'We're obeying our Masters: it's *your* debt we're paying
The price may be great, but the settlement's near.'

'Oh! Why are you droning, you Great Planes in Flanders,
Above with the stars, while my vigil is kept?'
'We are risking, and watching, and ever remember
Dead faces of babes who were slain as they slept.'

'Oh! Why are you bare, all you Great Trees of Flanders,
So naked and stark, and so battered and torn?'
''Twas the price that we paid when we gave of our beauty
To shelter and shield Sons that England has borne.'

'Oh! Why are you stricken, you Wide Lands of Flanders;
With great gaping wounds on your bosom so red?'
'Tread soft. No God's Acre was ever more holy:
Your Sons are at peace. We are guarding your dead.'

'Oh! Why are you toiling, you Women in Flanders;
There's work to be done, but the work isn't light;
There are sights which strike dumb, bodies broken and shattered;
Black Hell is let loose, and Grim Death rides at night?'

'Aye! We know it full well. Oh! the anguish past telling.
Dear God! Give us strength. Give us grace for our task.
The women these men love are praying in England
To heal and restore them is all that we ask.'

'Oh! Why not give in, Weary Men, out in Flanders,
Death lurks in the air and for you he has sought?'
'Give in? Are we craven? There's work to be finished.
Our eyes have beheld what the Devil has wrought!'

'Oh! Why are you lying there, Boy, out in Flanders—
A smile on your lips?' 'He has answered the call.
His strength was not great, but his spirit was mighty.
He offered his youth, but they robbed him of all.'

Dear Mother of God. Tell his mother in England
He paid the full price, but he paid with a smile.
He passed through the Vale with Thy Dear Son beside Him
And heard His 'Well Done': Surely that was worth while!

ANIMO ET FIDE

(Written by Mr. James Dimmock in April, 1918.)

Courage and Faith! That is the trumpet call
For those brave souls who suffer and endure,
And who, with steadfast eye and purpose sure,
Await the hour when good shall conquer all;
And though the fight be long, and dark the days,
And night's grim shattering menace rends the skies,
Shall to the call of duty sternly rise,
And fearlessly towards the future gaze.
For Faith shall bear them through the time of stress,
In certain knowledge of a better day;
And hope shall guide them on the troubled way,
Till Freedom comes to purify and bless;
And Courage shall be theirs to climb the height
Of all that men can do and dare for Right.

THE 1ST AND 3RD CITY OF LONDON (PRUDENTIAL) VOLUNTARY AID DETACHMENTS

At the beginning of 1918 our detachments were considerably below strength. The firing line needed every man of military age and fitness and those able to undertake ambulance work at home carried on under considerable difficulty.

Sincere appreciation of the work done by the V.A.D.s was expressed from time to time by officials from all quarters. On January 31st, Major Wilfred Brand, in charge of casualties in the London District, entertained the officers of the Ambulance Column to dinner. During the course of their visit Major Brand told the Commandants he had received many letters congratulating him on the loyal and devoted service of the detachments under his supervision. Amongst those who had written to him were the General Officer Commanding the London District and the Director General of the Army Medical Services. Major Brand gave instructions for the contents of the letters to be circulated to all members of the detachments.

On Friday, June 28th, Their Majesties King George V and Queen Mary, accompanied by Princess Mary (now the Princess Royal), visited Waterloo Station to watch detraining operations from an ambulance train. Lieut.-General Sir Francis Lloyd, and Lieut.-General A. MacDonald, D.D.M.S., were in attendance. Their Majesties passed through the train and talked with the wounded soldiers who were being transferred to the ambulances. Both the King and Queen afterwards expressed high appreciation of the splendid service rendered by the Ambulance Column.

To the end of October, 1918, the Column had evacuated over 4,500 trains and transferred some 612,000 casualties from station to hospital or from one hospital to another.

An interesting comment in connection with the V.A.D. was sent to us by Mr. E. J. Holker who writes :

'I had the rather remarkable experience of leaving an Advanced Dressing Station in France and finding myself a week later in a "Prudential" bed in a "Prudential" hospital under a "Prudential" doctor and waited on by a "Prudential" nurse. The hospital was the Finsbury Square V.A.D. Hospital maintained entirely by our Company. Of all the services rendered to the Country at that time by our Company that service was the most highly appreciated by those soldiers fortunate enough to get there.'

SIR EDGAR HORNE

In April, 1918, the present chairman of the Company, Sir Edgar Horne, paid a visit to France and made a tour of the Front.

CHIEF OFFICE MALE STAFF

Some interesting details of the War record of the Chief Office Staff of the Company are given in an Editorial in the August, 1918, issue of the *Ibis Magazine*. We quote it in full :

'With the month of August the nation enters on its fifth year of participation in the great conflict for freedom and public right. It is obviously impossible for contemporaries of the tremendous events to appreciate properly the momentous purport of the issues at stake : that can only be appraised by posterity with its truer perspective and its more detached outlook. But we can at least admire the courage and honour, the sacrifice of those who have gone forth for the defence of everything that England holds dear, and for the maintenance of her great traditions of liberty and justice. These four years of struggle have made great inroads on the Company's staff, but they have also evoked examples of unparalleled daring and distinguished service. We need not conceal a legitimate pride, not only in the initial response to the country's call, but also in the splendid record of achievement and distinction which our colleagues have attained. Some brief review of this may not be inappropriate on the eve of the fourth anniversary of the outbreak of war.

'The pre-war Chief Office Male Staff numbered 1,720, and the number of those who have joined the Forces since amounts to 1,288. This figure, of course, includes those junior members of the staff who have entered the Company's service since August, 1914. The number now actually serving is 1,110; 122 have given their lives, and 58 have been discharged from the Army as the result of wounds or illness contracted on service. Of those now serving, 22 hold commissions in the Royal Navy and 294 in the Army. Among the latter, there are included one Lieutenant-Colonel, 7 Majors, 45 Captains, 91 1st Lieutenants, and 150 2nd Lieutenants, while 31 are at present undergoing training in Cadet Schools. Of the men serving in the ranks, no fewer than 120 have become N.C.O.s'. This list is doubtless incomplete, as in many cases there is reason to believe no information has been received of advancement in the ranks of officers. Similarly, with regard to the decorations that have been earned, many of the recipients with natural modesty have been silent in regard to their decorations; but of those of which information has been received there are included: C.M.G., 1; D.S.O., 1; D.F.C., 1; M.C., 16; Bar to M.C., 1; M.M., 6; Albert Medal, 1; and 6 foreign decorations, comprising the Legion of Honour, the Croix de Guerre, and certain Russian Orders. Of the Ladies' Staff, a considerable number are attached to the Red Cross detachments who work on a rota, not less than 40 being engaged on service in hospitals at any one time. Six are serving in hospitals abroad and six work during the evenings—and when required, at night—with the Ambulance Column. Eight have joined the W.A.A.C.s and many others render valuable service as members of the Green Cross and kindred organizations. The work of the Men's Red Cross detachments is well known to readers of the Magazine.

'All this constitutes a record of service of which we may well be proud and do well to honour. But, above all, in this review of achievements of the past four years we needs must pay supreme tribute to those who have given their all, and have thereby rendered the greatest service which any man can give to his country. Their untimely death in the flower of manhood leaves us impoverished by their loss but enriched by the memory of the undying honour of their sacrificed service.'

THE WESTERN FRONT

When the campaign of 1918 opened the battle line on the Western Front ran in a southerly direction from a point near Ostend past Ypres, Lille, Lens and Cambrai to La Fere. From there it bent to the eastward passing Soissons, Rheims and Verdun and thence to the Swiss Frontier. On March 21st, 1918, the German troops over-ran the entire territory which the British and French had captured during the previous summer. On April 6th, however, the drive was at an end. Severe fighting broke out again on May 27th on the Aisne. The Germans overwhelmed the French position between Soissons and Rheims. The French slowly retreated and the battle-front was only 44 miles from Paris. The Germans started another drive on July 15th, but on July 18th the signal for an allied counter-attack was given. The Germans were quickly driven back and on August 2nd the French retook Soissons. On 8th August the British launched a great offensive in the Somme region. In little more than a month the Allies took 100,000 prisoners and the Germans were in full retreat on a front of 140 miles. The British, French, Belgian and American troops all pushed forward on their own fronts until November 11th, 1918, and by that time the Germans had practically been driven out of France and were retreating in confusion and despair.

Mr. H. J. Young acted as Commandant of the district between Amiens and Albert just as the final attack on the 8th August commenced. He says, 'Whilst with the battalion we had the disagreeable experience of holding the Passchendaele Front after the attack had finished. There were no trenches and no wire and we were enfiladed from both left and right, being in a sharp salient. There were no roads or tracks and the line held was simply a succession of wet shell holes. One man of my Company was actually drowned in the mud although we had drag ropes provided for pulling out any men who were unable to struggle out by themselves.'

Mr. Young joined the Volunteer Force in 1902; in 1912 he became Colour Sergeant in the 8th Essex Battalion; he was gazetted as 2nd Lieutenant on the 13th August, 1914; in September, 1914, he became Assistant Adjutant of the 2/8th Essex Battalion; in March, 1915, a third line Battalion was authorized and he was given command of this with the duty of raising and training the men. Subsequently he rejoined his first line Battalion and proceeded to France. He was given command of a Company and ultimately became Second in Command of the Battalion.

Mr. W. T. Owen as No. 1 Machine Gunner fought a rearguard action in the retreat on 22nd March when the Fifth Army retreated.

Mr. W. M. McKendrick's battery, 'C' Battery, 29th Brigade Royal Field Artillery, was the battery on the right of the English Sector facing La Fere, the extreme right of the line and remained with the Fifth Army right through the retreat to Amiens. He was one of the original members of this Battery to return home.

Mr. F. L. Jones was one of eight left out of the whole of his Machine Gun Company, all the others being killed or captured.

Mr. C. V. Alder, who was with the Fifth Army when the German Army broke through on the 21st March, was in contact with the enemy until wounded on 12th April.

Mr. A. Milledge, having wintered in Italy, returned to the Arras front in March, 1918. He was wounded and captured on Palm Sunday—24th March.

Mr. F. J. Roberts who was with the Third Army was in this German 'push'.

Mr. M. Martin tells us:

'An outstanding memory was our great retreat on the Western Front in 1918 when I was attached to a Flying Column of the Royal Field Artillery. We moved from point to point without relief for weeks on end, holding the weaker sections of our line and finally having to abandon some of our guns. Our horses and mules were shot from under us.'

Mr. C. D. Green, too, on the 22nd March, was ordered to abandon the guns. These, however, were ultimately recovered in spite of severe gun fire and bombardment from hostile aeroplanes.

Mr. F. C. Sawyer was among the Company of composite troops who fought the rear-guard action in March, 1918.

Others who participated in this general retirement were Messrs. R. G. Artesani, F. S. Bennett, H. Cooper, H. S. French, F. H. Garraway, L. J. Hawkins, E. M. Jones, S. J. May, J. O'Donnell, A. P. Perry, J. Perry, A. B. Smith, E. Spencer Smith, G. I. Smith,

P. H. Smith, V. G. Taylor, P. Thomason and E. T. Whittaker (who was wounded).

On 27th May the Battle of the Aisne commenced. Here Mr. G. J. Gould was taken prisoner after the 8th Division had been surrounded during the German attack.

From 15th–18th July the Second Battle of the Marne took place. Mr. B. T. Sayer, who had taken part in the March retirement, also took part in this battle.

From 8th August until September the Battle of Amiens raged with ultimate victory for the Allies. Both Mr. T. J. Demott and Mr. A. Onyett took part in this battle and in the subsequent advance. Others whom we have traced as having taken part in the final advance were Messrs. S. J. May, J. O'Donnell, A. P. Perry, B. T. Sayer, E. Spencer Smith and G. I. Smith, but this must be an infinitesimal proportion of the names which should rightly be included.

A further list of a few of those who served on the Somme during some period of 1918 is as follows:

H. W. Coates	A. S. Lawton	R. C. Stevenson
C. I. Gilham	R. E. Mallinson	E. H. Thomas
J. Glenn	G. W. Newell	S. Tuley
R. Hall	E. F. Poole	A. H. Wild
P. C. Hughes	S. S. Redgrove	H. J. Young

EXPLOSION ON H.M.S. *GLATTON*

Here is a first-hand description of the explosion on H.M.S. *Glatton* told by Mr. J. N. Shine. Mr. Shine was mobilized on 2nd August, 1914, from the Royal Naval Reserve, and demobilized in 1919 with the rank of Paymaster-Lieutenant. In 1914 he was engaged in patrolling north of the Shetlands and visited Russia. In 1915 he was mine-sweeping in H.M.S. *Lilacs*. On 18th August the ship was mined and abandoned in a heavy sea but was afterwards recovered. The disaster to H.M.S. *Glatton*, which he describes so graphically, occurred on 12th September, 1918, in Dover Harbour.

'The Admiralty announce that one of H.M. monitors was sunk in harbour on — — as a result of an internal explosion. One officer and 19 men were killed by the explosion, and 57 men are missing, presumed killed.'

'The above brief statement does not convey very much, and being one of those on board at the time, I have set down my own experience of an accident which does not usually leave many survivors.

'It was about six o'clock in the afternoon, and I had just gone into the Captain's cabin with the First Lieutenant to get him some confidential books, when we heard an explosion, and all the lights went out. Number One, being a man of action, was through the door and on the quarter-deck in a flash, while I stood hesitating with my hands full of books, wondering what had happened. A moment after came a shock like a collision and a rumbling roar, followed by showers of sparks and a blinding sheet of flame that seemed to fill the whole cabin. Then came a terrific crash and I thought the end of everything had come.

'The next I remember was picking myself up rather shakily from a corner some ten feet from where I had been standing. I expected to find the whole ship crumbling away after that fearful crash but the cabin was 150 feet away from the explosion, and beyond a lot of splintered woodwork, not much the worse. The chief force of the explosion was upwards, and those ashore said the flame shot up over 200 feet, while the flash ran right along the main deck to the extreme ends of the ship, bursting several bulkheads. One man saw the flash from a ship twenty-five miles away. Somewhat to my surprise I was practically unhurt, but my face felt on fire and I was a bit rocky on my legs. The Captain's ladder had vanished, and I made my way to the Ward-room one, but the flat was pitch-dark and full of smoke, so I came back and climbed out with some difficulty through the hatch. The quarter-deck was not much damaged, but a dense cloud of smoke was pouring out amidships and flames over 40 feet high were licking round the huge tripod mast, while the control top was blazing fiercely. The ship showed no sign of listing, and there seemed little immediate danger unless another magazine went, but I did not think of that at the time; my chief anxiety in such emergencies is confidential books and ledgers. As we were in one of our own harbours, there did not seem much cause for worry in the first instance, so I made for the ship's office.

'As soon as I got into the superstructure, I found it quite dark and filled with dense masses of suffocating smoke. I was nearly choked and was afraid to go on in the dark, so made for the open again. Later I found that the P.M.O. had more pluck and had actually managed to drag some men out without any help. On making a further attempt, he lost himself in the blinding smoke and getting near the flames, was frightfully burnt and injured. He lost all consciousness of what he was doing, but must have stumbled out again somehow without help, for there was no one else near. Number One got safely to the quarter-deck before the flames reached him, and was not injured, but he tried to fight his way forward through the smoke and was never seen again.

'After giving up the attempt to reach the ship's office, I tried to get down to my cabin for the other ledger, but the ladder down the Ward-room hatch had been blown away, while the Captain's ladder had been torn from its sockets and thrown on deck. With the help of the carpenter I was trying to get this down to the Ward-room, when I heard a call for help, and went over to the sky-light to lend a hand to some men who were climbing through. Not being able to see very clearly without my glasses, I caught at one chap's hands; he gave an awful groan, and I saw they were fearfully burnt and lacerated. We got him out by the shoulders, as well as two others. Then I heard a cry from the bottom of the gangway, and ran down to find a chap in the water who had been blown off the upper bridge and seemed too dazed to climb out. I helped him into a trawler's boat just coming alongside, and came back to find someone leading the gunner. He was the worst case I saw, though with help he could stumble along. The warning, "Lead him carefully, he's blind", was needless after one glance at his face, which had caught the full force of the flame. We got him into the boat, and came up again to see if there were any more, but by this time the deck was deserted, the others having climbed into a boat which was lying astern. We shouted down the hatch, but the flat below was quite dark and full of smoke, and seemed deserted. The trawler's boat was still alongside, so we got in and shoved off.

'There were still a lot of men on the fo'c'sle, but there were crowds of boats alongside, undeterred by the chance of a further explosion, so we made for the depot ship. On the way I began to realize that I was a bit the worse for wear. My hair and eyebrows were pretty well singed and full of charred splinters and matted with blood, though I had no recollection of being hit. Everyone was as black as a nigger with the smoke, and we were all so burnt and swollen that we could only recognize each other by our voices. It was probably the first sight of us as we came alongside that made them log us as seriously injured and send for our relatives, although after a week's careful dressing I was quite all right again.

'So much for my own experiences. Of the other officers, those below were blown about like chaff by the first blast of the explosion.

The steel bulkhead of the Ward-room was burst in two places, and one man blown through the gap. The chief engineer, who was in his cabin, was blown out into the flat and thrown down an open hatch, falling some ten feet on to his shoulder ; he managed to climb out, but sadly injured his scorched hands in doing so. All the lights went out, and the whole flat was filled with choking fumes. One poor fellow, groping for the ladder to the quarter-deck, fell down the hatch leading to the deck below, and only saved himself by catching at the guard-chains which were nearly red-hot. The gunner was sitting writing close to the door of his cabin, which opened obliquely on to the flat ; he caught the full force of the flame, and died from the effect of the burns a few days later. His cabin was next to mine, so I was lucky to be away at the time.

' Amidships, there must have been a veritable inferno of smoke and flame. There were some wonderful escapes, and many were blown out of the ship before the flame reached them, while others much further away succumbed to fearful burns. Some splendid work was done getting men out, but it was hard to get any details. I heard that one man who had got hold of a gas-mask made his way into the smoke eighteen times, dragging a man out each time. Everything possible was done to get the injured out of the ship, but in most cases they were past help. On board the depot ship, where they were bringing some of the injured, it was terrible. By that time my own burns were making me feel none too happy, but it was ten times worse listening to the groans of those who were really bad. Some who had been having a bath were burnt nearly all over, and nearly mad with pain, while about twenty died during the next few days from the effects of shock or burns. I suppose there are few injuries more painful than severe burns from which nearly all were suffering, and many could not use their hands for weeks afterwards.

' A previous experience of abandoning ship, in a heavy sea after being mined, seemed a small thing compared with the horrors of that day.'

OCTOBER 5TH, 1918

Mr. P. J. Carter, who was awarded the Military Medal in 1917 when with the Scots Guards, in a letter written in 1918 describes an unpleasant moment when trying to spot the position of a particularly destructive enemy post.

" . . . I pushed on towards the point, when I saw what I imagined was a gleam of light from a dug-out, and walked on confidently, as I knew only our people would be careless enough to exhibit a light in such an exposed position. When within fifteen yards of the place, I solved the phenomenon of the light, which was caused by the illuminating lights flung up by the Germans three or four miles away, on a flank, being visible through a railway-arch blown up by explosive, the remainder of the horizon being blanketed by the embankment twenty feet in height. Concurrently with this discovery I heard voices whispering behind a line of shrubs that fringed the swamp at the bottom of the embankment, and the sounds not seeming familiar I scented trouble, but challenged them in the normal way. No response, but more guttural murmuring, I called again ; the muttering ceased. Getting impatient, I flavoured my next query with a profane addition, and got ready for eventualities. I got them —machine-gun fire opened on me at fifteen yards, with a standing figure-target presented to the operator, who was situated on the top of the embankment, with me below. The fact of its being a machine-gun saved me, as I swear only one bullet passed me before I was flattened at the bottom of a shell-hole two yards away, which I had negotiated on my way up. Bullets pinged, machine-guns rattled, earth spat, rifles clicked, and I ceased to breathe. After a few minutes the pandemonium slackened somewhat, and fearing a bomb or two I took advantage of the spell and decamped forty yards at the double to the next shell-hole. More excitement for a minute, and I then navigated some barbed wire, with lamentable results to my habiliments, and streaked off for home and country. I attribute my escape to the fact that being an isolated post, the Germans were even more frightened than I was, and also to the fact that a machine-gun needs to be more carefully laid and sighted than a rifle, as it takes a good man to miss a standing figure at fifteen yards with small arms.'

AN 18 POUNDER AT CHIEF OFFICE

In October, 1918, a gun was brought to Chief Office. This was on the occasion of the 'Feed the Guns' campaign and followed the precedent established by the tank in October, 1917.

The gun in question was an 18 pounder drawn by six magnificent horses, and in the charge of a Lieutenant and four men of the R.F.A., all of whom had seen service at the Front. The visit occasioned a good deal of public interest, and a crowd of spectators awaited the arrival of the gun in the courtyard of the Chief Office, while the windows abutting on the courtyard were crowded with onlookers.

Sir Thomas Dewey received the visitors with a substantial cheque for £250,000 to feed the gun, which brought the Company's War Bonds up to nearly ten millions, and their total holdings in war securities at that time to £35,000,000.

'If you love your country', said Sir Thomas, at the conclusion of his remarks on handing over the cheque, 'lend your money at once to the Government, and so hasten the day when Peace shall be declared on a basis that shall free the world once and for all from German slavery and militarism.'

THE REAL HUMAN SIGNIFICANCE OF IT ALL

Towards the end of 1918 this letter was written by Mr. P. M. Stephens. It is extraordinarily interesting in the light of history. Note his last words. We think he was unduly pessimistic—yet who dare say that he was entirely wrong?

'. . . I have been slightly gassed but nothing bad, so shall be back in the line in a few days' time. I can't say much about our present operations, except that there is a very great difference in things since I was out here before. The absence of trenches is by no means an unmixed blessing. The countryside round here is not unlike that of England. When things are moving and nobody knows where anything is and the line which on newspaper maps appears so black and well-defined is invisible, then it is the easiest thing imaginable to walk into the view of an enemy sniper or machine-gunner. Of course, the recognized boy-scout stunt is to crawl along hedges on one's stomach, but as one has to go several miles sometimes to find a suitable observation-post this takes too long, so chances have to be taken. To-day I rode in a car for about seventy miles through the liberated districts; the desolation is too terrible for words. During a part of the ride we went for ten miles and saw hardly a square yard which is not a shell-hole or a trench. Houses, villages and towns are merely heaps of bricks and stones. The most awful aspect is the entire absence of civilian population. It is impossible for the English to appreciate the bitterness that the French people must feel to see their country so devastated and defiled. We saw ample evidence of German "frightfulness" apart from that which would be in any way necessitated by war. Acres of orchards have been destroyed, while less valuable bushes and trees in the immediate vicinity have been untouched in the hurried retreat. I am at present billeted in what was a beautifully furnished villa; every mirror has been wilfully smashed, and the piano also has been broken inside. However, it seems that at last the Huns are going to get their deserts; but I think that English people who have not seen the wreck that the Hun has made will soon forget the facts. Unfortunately no photos or pictures can ever do justice to the horror of it all. I suppose, after the war, a small proportion of the English will make trips to see the battle-fields, but the moss will then have grown over the ruins, and the trenches will be a mass of weeds and wild vegetation, and they will then appear to those tourists to have been the scene of some vast romantic struggle. Those who come after will not appreciate the innumerable domestic tragedies and disasters which lie hidden beneath; the real human significance of it all they will not comprehend. It is a pity—for the purifying and regenerating influence of the War will be largely lost on England.'

NOVEMBER 11TH, 1918

Throughout this book we have endeavoured to reconstruct the events of the War through the eyes of Prudential men who actually participated in these events.

Here then is a picture of November 11th, 1918, in London, written on the day itself by a member of the Chief Office Staff:

'Let us try to set down our impressions of this wonderful day, now slipping quietly to its close, with the picture vividly before us and the events fresh in our memory. This morning the news for which we had waited so long came swiftly, mysteriously, silently. At one moment all was normal: the next, groups of people were talking excitedly—the air seemed charged with emotion. "The Armistice has been signed and firing ceases at eleven o'clock, and my husband is coming home and I am going to buy a flag", said a lady breathlessly as she disappeared down the stairs. A gentleman was playing football with an old waste-paper basket, and flags were being festooned round the lamps. The maroons banged and clattered overheard. For a brief second we experienced the old dismal, sinking, here-they-are-again feeling, but only for a second, and then exultation held us in its sway. We looked out of the windows on to Brooke Street, and down it swarmed the girls from the Approved Society, laughing, running, waving little flags. Where the flags came from is a mystery. We all thought there was not a flag in London, and yet they sprang up in millions. Everybody had a flag and everybody waved it. Everybody cheered everybody else. The people who swarmed the buses—loading the tops, sides, and mudguards—cheered the people in the streets, and the people in the streets cheered the buses. They waved and shouted . . .

'A little girl dressed in black was sitting at her desk crying her heart out; and a father who had lost both his sons squared his shoulders and was silent. . . . The news spread that the Manager would address the staff in the courtyard, and we all surged out. We packed the courtyard and overflowed on to the railings, cheering and waving our flags, while the startled pigeons circled round and round overhead. The Red Cross bus stood in the middle, a tiny island in a sea of upturned faces. When the Manager appeared on the summit we cheered. The Manager spoke. He told us of the ten thousand Prudential men who had helped to bring this mighty triumph to pass. He reminded us solemnly of those who would never return, and we were hushed. . . . Then "God Save the King" welled up—a spontaneous anthem. We surged out of the gates into Holborn—Holborn transformed into a place of joy, for at last the dream of peace had become gloriously true. . . .

'To-night the searchlights stab the sky and we leave the curtains of our windows open so that the light may shine forth on the passers-by. To-morrow we will rub the black off our street-lamps and take up our lives once more; but to-night joy has made us tired. Let us say our prayers and go to bed and remember the dear ones who have fallen.'

And a poem from James Dimmock whose son was dead.

Victory

Bravely the bugles blow, and loud the beat
Of throbbing drums and clash of pealing bells,
The song of triumph to a chorus swells
With undertone of tramp of marching feet.
Back from the War! Back from the War they come,
From scenes of carnage and of ghastly strife;
To peace and beauty and the quiet life,
And all the joys that make a happy home.
But stretched on beds of misery and pain,
Blinded and maimed and stricken with disease,
Praying to God for merciful release,
A martyred host long agonies sustain.
While near and far, o'er battlefields wide-spread,
Our boys—our dear, beloved boys—lie dead!

DEMONSTRATION AT CHIEF OFFICE

Here is the official description of the demonstration in the courtyard :

The great courtyard, more than once in the history of the Great War, has been thronged with our Staff, intent on some great occasion, but never in its history has it witnessed such scenes of enthusiasm as were enacted at mid-day on the 11th November, in response to a managerial desire to meet us for a purpose which was not stated. From every point of egress the Staff poured into the courtyard ; from every window protruded heads (and bodies, at some risk) ; and around the Red Cross Conveyance—which has performed such noble service daily and nightly for the benefit of our wounded soldiers—the crowd was densest, and the waving flags thickest.

To this appropriate standpoint the General Manager made his way amidst a frenzy of excitement and applause, and from its roof addressed the assembly in the following words. His impressiveness communicated itself to his hearers, and the proceedings were marked by an earnestness which showed that all present realized the solemnity of the great historic occasion :

'The whole world is rejoicing today, and nobody has a greater right to rejoice than you have.

'I will tell you why. We have sent from this business 10,000 men to join in active service. We have sent quite a number of ladies as Nurses, and all of us have sent our sons, our brothers, or may be our lovers.

'Some of us have suffered. . . . We are glad to look forward to the return of those who come back uninjured in the prime of life.

'I will mention another reason why you are entitled to rejoice. It is because you have all through this period fulfilled your duty.

'The business we carry on here is very important business. As I bear the chief administrative burden I know what I am talking about. You are entitled to your rejoicing for helping to carry us through. You will, I know, not now let us down.'

Mr. Thompson then called upon those present to join him in singing the National Anthem.

In the afternoon a Service of Thanksgiving was held at St. Alban's, Holborn, which had been specially arranged for members of the Staff. A large congregation completely filled the beautiful church and the service was conducted by the Vicar, the Rev. H. Ross.

ARMISTICE DAY IN FRANCE

Here are two descriptions of Armistice Day written by Prudential men at the time.

This from Mr. E. R. Bushell:

'. . . The attack was successful beyond expectations, and by evening the infantry were beyond our maximum range (6,500 yards). Fortunately our Brigade was not called upon to go forward in close support of the infantry. The next four days we spent in bringing in captured guns and moving up dumps and making up detachments with reinforcements. During these four days I regret to say that the Colonel was killed. He had gone forward to see the Colonel of the Brigade we were going to relieve; they were walking down the road when a 4·2 arrived, killing both of them. It was very bad luck as he was going on leave next day. My Major, being senior Major in the Brigade, had to take over command of the Brigade, and I carried on with the Battery. We moved on and relieved another Army Brigade. We lived in a cellar and had a piano, so were quite comfortable, remaining for six days while the push, which afterwards turned out to be the last of the War, was prepared. During the six days I reconnoitred all the country in front and to a flank, and during those rides the contrast of peace and war was extraordinary. But for dead horses and Boches lying about I might have been riding through the lanes of Essex. The infantry had gone forward so quickly over this ground that comparatively little damage had been done. The break-up of the Boche morale was everywhere apparent; machine-guns, equipment, rifles, ammunition, etc., had been abandoned intact, and no attempt made to destroy it.

'The new Colonel arrived the night we went into action, but at my request the Major left the show to me. It was quite a picnic; I don't think we had half a dozen rounds near us all the time we were firing barrage. That afternoon and the next day the R.A.F. reported they could not find the Boche. Rumours at once began to fly about, especially as we had had official news about Bulgaria and Austria. We then got news about the German delegates coming through the French lines just south of us, but nobody believed it. We again moved forward, this time through the forest, and occupied a position near the eastern outskirts. The Major had again taken up the reins and I went back to waggon lines. And then the news, which we all fervently hoped might be right but dared not believe, came through verbally that the German delegates were given to 11 o'clock on the 11th to sign. At 8 o'clock on the 11th, an order came from G.H.Q. that hostilities would cease at 11 o'clock. I think we were all too amazed at what the news meant to give any expression to our feelings. However, at 10.58 all guns were loaded, and with the Major at No. 1 and myself at No. 2 (I was specially sent for), and with an officer at each of the other guns, we fired the last salvo at five seconds to eleven at the order of the B.S.M. For twenty-four hours afterwards we could hardly realize the War was really over. Everybody lit bonfires, and the R.A.F. sent up rockets, but the troops did not create as much noise as we expected.'

Mr. R. C. Pettingale gives the following description of happenings in Rouen :

'. . . All the bells pealed, and the syrens of numerous vessels on the Seine sounded, and regular pandemonium prevailed. Anything at all resembling a band was immediately requisitioned. Nearby hospitals and camps organized huge processions of Australians, Americans, Nursing Sisters, and W.A.A.C.s, and with soldiers dressed in German uniforms (hastily acquired from neighbouring compounds), with chains and halters round their necks, they toured the town. All restraint was entirely abandoned, dignified Colonels were caught up and swirled into the procession, flags thrust into their hands, and they were freely embraced by the local French " ladies ". It was a never-to-be-forgotten scene. One incident amused me greatly. In the afternoon I met a chum of mine in the street, a man in charge of a hospital ward of 40 beds. Upon my asking him how he managed to get away at a moment's notice, he replied, " Well, all my *bed patients* have got up and gone out, so what is the use of *my* staying there ? " '

Mr. C. J. Gratton possesses a souvenir. It is a streamer dropped on his Battery just outside Ath whilst in open action. It is a pouch attached to long streamers, blue, red and yellow, dropped from an aeroplane ordering the Battery to cease fire as the Armistice had been signed.

Mr. W. J. Glendenning represented the 64th Company, Royal Garrison Artillery, at a Durbar in Rangoon where the Peace Proclamation was read in English, Hindustani and Burmese.

When the Armistice was signed, Mr. C. F. Menage was reconnoitring with a party over the River Scheldt looking for ' booby ' traps and mines. It was 12 o'clock midnight before he heard the news. Clay pipes 14 inches long were handed round to smoke in celebration.

Mr. R. H. Wacey had the pleasure of announcing to 1,000 German prisoners that the Armistice had been signed.

Mr. A. C. Wylie was on telephone duty in Belgium and took the message that hostilities had ceased, a copy of which is among his souvenirs.

NOVEMBER, 1918. FROM THE DIRECTORS TO THE STAFF

Thanks be to God, the protracted hostilities have at length ceased, and Victory has crowned the courage, the strategy and the endurance displayed in their righteous cause by Great Britain and her Allies. The magnificent record of our nation is the aggregate of the efforts made by all classes of our people—so, too, the splendid achievements of the Prudential consist of those things which have been done individually or collectively by those associated with the Company in whatever capacity.

The Directors tender their most cordial thanks to everyone who has during the War done her or his best to overcome the unprecedented difficulties of the situation, and thus to enable the Company to 'carry on'. It is a wonderful record which the Company has to hand on to future generations, and we believe that in days long distant the action of the Prudential in relation to the problems and difficulties presented by the war will be applauded as having contributed effectively to the welfare of the State, and as having greatly enhanced the reputation of the Company.

The strain on the Company has been without parallel in its history, and though it will be sensibly relaxed in a few weeks or months, some time must elapse before the effects will have entirely passed away. The necessity for sustained effort does not end with the War: we are confronted with problems of reconstruction throughout the country, and also at Holborn Bars, and our success, alike in times of peace or war, will be in proportion to the contribution we can make to the welfare of the community.

It is essential that our Company should continue to lead in reducing the expense of administering the business: good progress in organizing towards this end has been made during the War, and in future years the result will be clearly seen. The staff at Chief Office can help enormously in this direction by developing and encouraging a spirit of cheerful efficiency throughout all the departments, and by acquainting themselves with the standards of excellence attained in divisions other than their own, with the object of equalling or excelling them. Economy in administration creates increased opportunity for remunerating efficient work, and the Directors were never more mindful than now of the interests of their staff.

They thank their officers and staff again for unwavering loyalty and help. They wish them a Merry Christmas and a Happy New Year, and the best of good fortune in the future.

THE 1ST AND 3RD CITY OF LONDON (PRUDENTIAL) VOLUNTARY AID DETACHMENTS

Although the Armistice and cessation of hostilities in November brought with it a temporary lull in work, the subsequent arrival of large numbers of casualties from French hospitals and from the East kept our V.A.D. units well occupied for a further three months. On December 8th alone, eleven trains were met and some 1,310 wounded transferred.

On December 12th members of the Prudential Detachments assisted in the embarkation of American wounded on s.s. *Saxonia* at Tilbury. A letter of thanks and appreciation of their help was subsequently received by the Deputy Director of the London Ambulance Column. The writer—Colonel F. A. Washburn, Chief Surgeon of the American Expeditionary Forces—concludes with the paragraph: 'I want to thank Mr. Symons for making the arrangements, and Mr. Simmons for carrying them out, and will you please thank, on behalf of both the American Service and myself, all the members of the Ambulance Column who took part.'

The last Ambulance train was evacuated on 31st March, 1919, and the detachments were demobilized three months later, in June.

In recognition of their services during the War, Commandants W. F. Symons and F. V. Simmons were awarded the O.B.E. and M.B.E. respectively.

In conclusion we quote below the text of a resolution passed at a meeting of the City of London Branch of the British Red Cross Society, held at the Mansion House on the 20th April, 1920.

GUILDHALL,
LONDON.

Final War Meeting of the City Branch of the British Red Cross Society, held at the Mansion House under the presidency of the Lady Mayoress, April 20th, 1920.

Resolution—moved by Lieut.-General Sir Francis Lloyd, K.C.B., C.V.O., D.S.O., seconded by Major-General Sir Geoffrey Feilding, K.C.B., C.M.G., D.S.O. :
'That the gratitude of the City of London, as represented by this Meeting of the City of London Branch of the British Red Cross Society, be expressed to all the officers and members of the Ambulance Column, the Tilbury Column, and the Hospital Service Unit, for their magnificent work in their various departments during the Great War, 1914–19. Thanks and acknowledgments are also tendered to the V.A.D.s, both men and women, who staffed the hospitals during that anxious time. The arduous work of all, and especially of the Ambulance Column, was done with efficiency and self-sacrifice. It met with the warm approval of the military authorities, and this meeting desires to add its meed of praise for the devotion displayed by all ranks.

CHARLOTTE L. COOPER,
Lady Mayoress, *President.*
RICHARD DAVIES, *Chairman.*
M. C. GOODHUE, *Secretary.*

CHRISTMAS

For the last time, the Directors and Principal Officers sent letters of greeting to our members on Service and to our Red Cross workers, which letters were accompanied by a gift of chocolate, as in preceding years. These letters were as follows :

Christmas, 1918.

DEAR ——,

Once again—and I doubt not for the last time—I have the opportunity of conveying to Prudential men on Active Service the hearty admiration and the ever-growing confidence of their colleagues of all ranks at home. Our admiration is compelled by knowledge of sacrifices endured without complaint, and the hardened resolution with which our men, in common with their other British and Allied comrades, are rapidly breaking the evil spirit of enemy nations. Events are hastening towards the end, and as I write these words the military despotism which sought the enslavement of the world is tottering to its fall.

In many replies to my earlier letters, I have noted with satisfaction expressions of unchanging reliance on the triumph of our righteous cause, and I have often been told, 'I could say much more but for the Censor.' I have now to confess that *I* could say much more but for the Paper Controller, but the one thing we hope you will always cherish in your recollection, is the great satisfaction which the Company has felt in bearing some of the financial burdens which would have pressed heavily on many of those of our colleagues who have joined the colours.

The decision of our Government to release first of all at the close of the War those whose civilian positions are being kept open for them, leads us to hope that we may be able to welcome you back to the work of the old Company at no distant date, and in the meantime we join in sending you the warmest greetings for Christmas and the New Year.

Believe me,
Ever sincerely yours,
A. C. THOMPSON.
General Manager.

Christmas, 1918.

DEAR ——,

The Prudential Voluntary Aid Detachments of the British Red Cross Society have completed another year of splendid work since last I had the pleasure of writing to you, and I want you to realize how proud we are of the courage and endurance which have enabled you, in spite of almost overwhelming difficulty, to carry on your noble work of rendering succour to those who have been wounded and broken in our country's cause.

You have earned and received, first of all, the gratitude of those whose sufferings and hardships you have so cheerfully and persistently sought to relieve; you have helped to win for the British Red Cross Society the approbation of King and Country and the admiration of all that is best throughout the world, and in gaining the distinction which always rewards the efficient and self-sacrificing performance of good deeds, you have brought honour to the Company and to those who are associated with you as colleagues.

Writing on behalf of the Company and all your colleagues, I wish you a Happy Christmas and the best of New Years.

Believe me,
Ever sincerely yours,
A. C. THOMPSON.
General Manager.

PRISONERS OF WAR

Men who spent long and weary months in prison camps had difficulty in filling in their time and many of them sought relief in writing. It happens therefore that although in our search for original letters and documents of the war years we have sometimes been disappointed in the scarcity of the available material, we have had an *embarrassment of riches* in the experiences of prisoners of war. So many diaries were kept that it would have been possible to fill a whole volume with them. The necessity of confining the story to one chapter has made it impossible for us to make use of most of the material available. We have, therefore, selected several extracts in the hope that in giving the history of the few we are indicating the experiences of the many.

First we give a dramatic account by Mr. W. Allan of how he fell into German hands. It was on the morning of the 22nd August, 1917, and our troops had just attacked near the Menin Road.

'I foresaw', writes Mr. Allan, 'that we should have difficulty in holding out against the counter-attack. Some time later, an officer called me to join him and bring some grenades. Picking up a bag of bombs I hurried over the intervening ground. Half-way across I received a serious body wound and dropped into the nearest shell-hole. I was again struck on the left arm. After that things became hazy. I remember wading through the chalky water, waist high. I remember the morning light changing gradually to a wintry grey. Then with appalling suddenness came inky darkness and I fell forward and knew no more.

'A sound wakened me. It was a British aeroplane circling slowly overhead. I sat up. Everything appeared fairly quiet saving an odd sniper here and there. I realized it was afternoon as the sun was towards the West. With infinite difficulty I managed to get out my field-dressing. I could do nothing for my arm, the body wound was my immediate attention. Strange what a bullet will do. The bullet had passed through the leather equipment of my trenching tool, then turning had ripped along the lower part of the abdomen and ploughed its way through the hollow of the leg, finally coming out in front of the right thigh and leaving a hole about the size of a halfpenny. I had scarcely finished when the click of a rifle-bolt caused me to look up. It was a German soldier with his rifle pointed at me. I made the sign for a drink. The soldier smiled and sliding down into the hole gave me a drink of cold coffee. Then pointing to the opening of the shell-hole he kept saying "Kamerad". I understood. Creeping out I found a wounded British soldier lying on his face. I could see no blood. When he said he had no pain, but couldn't get up owing to the weight of his equipment, I guessed his wound was mortal. I helped to find water, which he drank greedily. Then I ventured into the open. I knew there were snipers about, but my desire for water was paramount. I had noticed a dead British soldier some little way ahead, and half crawling, half running I set out to get his water-bottle, but a sniper took a shot at me. I heard the crack just as I reached my objective and a bullet seared my left side as with hot iron. I fell on the dead man, and lay still. After a while I succeeded in crawling back with the precious bottle. Suddenly my comrade passed away and I was left alone . . .' Night came and Mr. Allan took cover in a sniper's post. Suddenly a German appeared, ordering him out. A shell burst close by, smashing the sniper's post and killing the German. Mr. Allan again lapsed into unconsciousness. '. . . When I awoke the morning was bright and sunny. All I wanted was water. My left arm was throbbing violently, as the bullet was imbedded in the bone. Crawling along I came upon a wounded German who like myself was cut off. He bandaged my arm, while I helped to staunch a bad wound in his head. He kept pointing to a German block-house some distance away for me to come with him. I shook my head, as I hoped to get back to my own lines. After a while the German got to his feet and started running across "No Man's Land". A little way over he was killed by a shell. Towards evening as I lay listlessly watching the setting sun and wondering if I should live to see its return, my attention was drawn to a German waving a Red Cross flag from a shell-hole just out of the zone of fire and inviting me over. I felt I could not reach it in my weakened condition. I lay for a moment debating which course to adopt. Behind (to the British lines), was a sea of fire, and return was hopeless.

1918

THE BRITISH TIMES

Edited and Printed for the British Prisoners of War at Schneidemühl.
Editor: F. E. Fisher

Printed and Published under the direction of The British Help Committee. Schneidemühl.

Nov. 16th, 1918. The Official Organ of The British Help Committee.

ADVICE AND AN APPEAL

For the information of all our readers, and particularly for those on Kommando, we print overleaf an exhortation which has been received from the Council of Workmen and Soldiers and which they wish to be made known to all prisoners.

In doing so, we cannot too strongly emphasise the importance of all men complying with the request to follow the instructions contained therein and to refrain from all acts which are subversive to good order and discipline.

Many difficulties have to be overcome—means of transport to be found, arrangements to be made with neutral countries for our reception, the ensurement of the food supply and accommodation, and the thousand and one considerations which must attend the moving of vast numbers of men and material. The difficulties are being met with and the arrangements are being made and in all good time we shall find ourselves en route for home.

With the feeling of excitement and the desire to be on the move, the impatience of the slightest delay and the inclination to anticipate events—feelings, all of which are very natural at a time like the present—we are in complete sympathy. But no good purpose would be served, the end brought no nearer, by impulsive or unconsidered action of any kind.

We therefore urge you to be patient for yet a little while, remain at your task however irksome it may seem, and by so doing, assist the authorities, whose hands are full.

C. S. M. McMillan.
do. Hobson.
do. Whitfield.
Col. Sgt. Hayles.
British Committee at Schneidemühl.

[*Reproduction of a copy of the British Times in the possession of Mr. P. Liversedge*]

BRITISH HELP COMMITTEE NOTES.

All our readers will be sorry to hear of the undermentioned deaths which have occurred since our last publication:

No.	Rank	Name	Rgt.	Date	Place
30461	Pte.	Brittle, W.	1st K.O.Y.L.I.	14.9	Mannheim.
4847	Pte.	Munn, G.	53rd A.I.F.	15.10	Stargard.
3040	Pte.	Mahoney, B. J.	24th R. Fus.	17.10	
10091	Pte.	Green, A.	1st S. Staffs	22.10	
202149	L. Cpl.	Cummins, H. C.	1st 4th Lincolns	30.10	Konigst.
7197	Pte.	Bullock, T. H.	9th D.L.I.	31.10	Westkaseum.
7932	Pte.	Hughes, J.	1st S. Guards	2.11	Plötker.
462	Pte.	Wilson, G.	1st B. Watch	2.11	,,
6736	Pte.	Craig, T.	1st S. Guards	2.11	,,
65043	Pte.	Worthington, A. E.	12-13 N. Fus.	4.11	,,
235615	Pte.	Ashley, A.	5th W. Yorks	5.11	,,
23331	Pte.	Rice, J.	7th N. & D.	6.11	,,
16335	Pte.	Graham, A. E.	8th R. Bgde.	7.11	,,
35418	Pte.	Jordan, E. J.	8th Borders	8.11	,,
202353	Pte.	Gemmell, J. M.	14th Manchrs.	8.11	,,
23306	Pte.	Williams, H.	2nd D.L.I.	8.11	,,
34185	Pte.	Brown, E.	12th Midsx.	9.11	,,

On behalf of all ranks, letters of sympathy have been sent to their relatives, who will deeply feel the great loss of their loved ones. Among the above will be noticed some of our 1914 men. The ribbons taken from the wreaths after burial have also been sent. In all cases, all available ranks turned out to follow them to their last resting place.

An application has been made to all comrades to come to the financial assistance of the above interments.

§ § §

Owing to so many fresh arrivals in the lager, many of whom are wounded, and many others suffering from Spanish Grippe, the Committee find it impossible, at present, to help all men on A. K. with medical comforts, but as soon as fresh supplies arrive from home, their requests will be immediately dealt with.

§ § §

Sgt. Phelan has asked me to make it known to all men on A. K., who have written to him for writing material, that owing to printing difficulties, it has not been possible to meet all demands. He has now received the required amount, and will forward all requirements at once.

§ § §

The B. H. C. wish to make it known that after all expenses have been defrayed, all surplus monies of the British Times and B. H. C. will be handed over to assist the Central Prisoners of War Committee's Fund. All ranks are heartily thanked for their past invaluable co-operative assistance.

G. S. Hayles,
Col. Sgt., R. Ms.
President.

B. H. C. FURTHER NOTES.

A Memorial Cross will be erected, 4 ft. 10 in. high, by comrades to the memory of Cpl. M. W. Smith who died at Gross Born Lager. It is executed in polished white Saxony marble with suitable inscription cut and gilded by Pte. W. O. Davies. This will be sent to Gr. Born early next week.

§ § §

With reference to the late Pte. Cantrill who died on Commando, Cpl. Morris of the Scots Gds. has kindly undertaken, with his comrades' help, to arrange for the erection of a cross to the memory of same, at the cemetery where he lies buried.

AN OFFICIAL NOTICE.

Comrades,

The old German Government has ceased to exist. The actual Government, which is represented here by the Council of Workmen and Soldiers, succeeded in obtaining an armistice with the powers of the Entente, and there is no doubt that a definite Peace will be concluded before long.

We are prepared to send you home as soon as circumstances will permit and we are confident you will give us all possible aid in carrying through our intention. You will easily understand that a quick and undisturbed conveyance of all prisoners can only be attained if everybody keeps quiet and waits until his turn comes. We request you, therefore, to keep order and remain at your respective places until you are warned to be shifted. You have waited patiently for so many years and we trust you will continue to do so for a few weeks more. All your letters, parcels etc. will be forwarded to the working commandos in the usual way until the men are called back to the camp. Circumstances do not permit to call back all prisoners at once, as the organisation of the camp is not such that can harbour and nourish simultaneously all its English, French, Russian, Polish, Italian, Portuguese and Roumanian prisoners.

We repeat: Have patience and wait!

Do not attempt to leave your commando without official permission! It would be too dangerous for you. Remember that the food which you will be able to carry with you will not last for more than two or three days, and that it would be impossible to obtain more food on the road. Marauding and pillaging would be the only means to get food and we trust to your good sense as shown up till now, in not falling in with such an idea. You know that in such a case you are liable to be arrested and shot on the spot. On the other hand, prisoners who are arrested for mutiny or flight, will have to stay here until all the other prisoners have gone.

Don't act heedlessly! You will mix up everything and create a chaos, an anarchy which would follow your trail and would not stop at the borders of your own country. A general famine would break out under which you would have to suffer as well as everybody else.

The terms of the Armistice accepted by Germany are very severe. Germany, however, is quite willing to carry them through; but there are great technical difficulties to overcome. We must withdraw our armies, we must send food for the troops of the Entente which are going to occupy the western districts of our country, as food is very scarce there. We will have to convey hundreds of thousands of prisoners within the limited space of a few weeks. It will be impossible to carry this through if you do not assist us in the manner mentioned above. Therefore: Remain where you are and don't make any trouble or cause disaster.

Many of you have been in captivity three or four years, and we trust you will be able to stand it a few weeks more. The German government has the ardent desire to send you home without unnecessary delay. It will only be able to do so if you lend a helping hand and do your duty until your turn comes.

Schneidemühl, Nov. 14th, 1918.
KOMMANDANTUR
The Council of Workmen and Soldiers.

In front there was a fire-zone limited in extent, and a block-house in view. I determined to risk it. Crawling and running alternately I reached the shell-hole, but just as I was sliding into it a bullet passed through my right shoulder. Luckily it proved a flesh-wound only. When I got to the block-house I found it was occupied by a company of Saxons and they treated me kindly.'

ARRIVING AT A PRISON CAMP AT LILLE

This extract is taken from a book written by Mr. R. Walbancke and Mr. W. S. Casserley after their return to England. It was never published but was circulated privately amongst their friends. This experience was Mr. Casserley's. He describes how he and a party of British prisoners reached a fort. This is the sight which met their eyes.

' . . . We pulled up automatically with a sudden jerk, absolutely appalled by the dreadful sights and sounds that burst without warning upon our startled senses.

' In front of us were sixteen cells, in shape reminiscent of railway-arches, eight on the ground-level and eight above. All we could see at the moment was that the end of each dungeon had been partially bricked-up, leaving a small iron grating in the centre through which light and air could penetrate to some extent the gloomy interior. But it was not the cells themselves that chilled the blood in our veins and struck such terror into our hearts as to cause a feeling of physical nausea. It was the white-faced, dishevelled wretches in khaki who thronged to the bars and greeted us with shrill and cracked voices—dreadful and ominous caricatures of men, a living portrait-gallery of ourselves-to-be.

' *This*, then, was our destination.'

VARYING CONDITIONS

In the different prisoner of war camps conditions varied. Whilst some spent their time in hideous confinement and unrelieved monotony of work and hunger, others were able to enjoy, in some small degree, the interests and privileges of civilization.

Mr. G. F. Swaby, who was a prisoner at Groudenz, says : ' We formed ourselves into classes of an educational nature such as Book-keeping, Languages, Chemistry and Farming. It certainly helped to pass away the dreary days.'

Mr. S. S. Redgrove, who was at Heuberg, tells us that the Germans provided a hut for amusement. 'This was nicknamed the "Heuberg Palace", and on most Sundays some sort of show would be given. A number of the men had been prisoners up here for a long period and had in various ways accumulated theatrical costumes and musical instruments. With the coming of our big party a meeting was held and it was decided to arrange, so far as was possible, alternate English and French programmes. I was asked, with another corporal, to take over the business side. We had to fix up the tickets of admission, sell them and arrange the seating, which was quite a delicate matter as the seats were all one price. Later a balance-sheet had to be prepared. The profits were devoted to buying what dainties could possibly be obtained by direct or indirect means and taking them up to the hospital. In addition I would help with the "make-up" and occasionally take a part in the show.'

Mr. Redgrove also tells us that sports were occasionally organized. During the time he was there the British camp was wonderfully healthy and only one English funeral took place. This was of a sergeant who, in attempting to escape, contracted pneumonia.

Mr. A. Challis was a prisoner on an island in the Baltic—Danholm—a ferry journey from Stralshund. Educational classes and games were organized for the studious and energetic. On one occasion artists, painters and staff staged Bernard Shaw's 'Arms and the Man'. They had an exhibition of pictures and published a paper called *The Outlook*. There was a great deal of first-class talent available and thus the dreary hours were whiled away.

Mr. H. J. Southgate, taken prisoner after Easter, 1917, went to a prison camp at Limburg-an-Lahn. After a time the prisoners congregated together in the evening and organized community singing. They then formed a concert committee of which Mr. Southgate was a member and, clubbing together the stamps which they had as payment, purchased a piano. They also had an international orchestra, gave dramatic entertainments and had two nigger minstrel shows in which Mr. Southgate played the bones. There was a camp church for the use of each nationality in their own particular religion and, on two occasions, a Church of England clergyman visited the camp, once at Christmas when carols were sung. This camp possessed also a library.

CHRISTMAS DAY

Some prisoners of war were able to make the best of Christmas Day—for others their lot was indeed hard. Here are two heart-breaking experiences. The first is from Mr. W. S. Casserley:

'It was particularly cold on Christmas Day, which made the absence of fuel still more noticeable. A very gloomy day and darkness fell at about three o'clock. Our rations did not arrive until six in the evening and consisted of stinking fish-roe soup, so salt that we could scarcely swallow it, and rotten potatoes boiled in their jackets!

'The situation was retrieved to some extent later in the evening by one of the few Englishmen with us. This man had contrived to get out of quarantine into the main camp and whilst there secure a parcel. He returned in triumph with his riches concealed beneath his overcoat. On examining his parcel he found that it contained cigarettes but no tobacco, and we persuaded him to sell us a tin of salmon for a mark so that he could buy some tobacco later on. When we opened the tin we found that the liquid in it had frozen completely solid and we had to dig out the contents! All we could do was to leave the fish on our plates until it partially thawed, and then make our meal—rather a cold one for Christmas Day, but not to be sneered at in our circumstances. We lay in bed talking for some time after this excitement was over, and then turned over and sought sleep as a refuge from this dreary travesty of Christmas.'

Mr. W. Allan was in Cologne on Christmas Day, 1917. For him, also, this was a day far removed from festivity. He and some forty odd prisoners were earmarked for a parade through the streets of the city, while the people crowded the footpaths to jeer and laugh as they passed along. At noon the prisoners were marched to a military barracks for a plate of cabbage soup and a piece of black bread, their first food for over twenty-four hours.

FOOD

Many prisoners of war in the early days suffered terribly from hunger and their whole existence revolved round the question of food. They could think of nothing else because they were starving to death. Men at work would wander afield and devour anything they could find, such as raw cabbage leaves, swedes, mangel-wurzels and beans. A potato, if found, was deemed a luxury. On one occasion a party of men were returning from work when they met a farmer carting away a dead horse for burial. By arrangement with him and with the Germans our men took possession of this horse. They cut off steaks to be cooked when they returned to their billets and others, more unrestrained, began to eat the flesh raw. Soon the horse was stripped to the bones. This incident is vouched for by Mr. Casserley and Mr. Walbancke.

The news of the plight of our men reached this country, and in the course of time elaborate arrangements were made for the dispatch of parcels. The activities of the Prudential ladies in this connection is of interest.

PRISONERS OF WAR FUND

This Fund was started by the Ladies' Staff in May, 1915, and on the 24th of that month parcels were dispatched to three prisoners whose names had been obtained from the Central Committee as badly in need of assistance, and by the end of June, eight prisoners were receiving parcels. After that the number steadily increased.

Each prisoner on the Fund had a weekly parcel sent him. The following is a typical example :

1 lb. of margarine, ¼ lb. of tea, ½ lb. of sugar, tin of milk (small), tin of beef, tin of tomatoes, tin of pears, tin of salmon, tin of golden syrup, cigarettes. There were also sent scarves, socks, mittens, handkerchiefs, and, at Christmas, plum pudding, tinned turkey, soup, shortbread, tin of biscuits, 1 lb. of chocolate, toffee and home-made cake.

At first the ladies made up the parcels themselves, but under new Government regulations, all parcels for prisoners had to be sent through Central or Regimental Committees ; the name and address of the 'adopter' was put inside the parcel to keep up the personal interest.

The new system ensured every prisoner receiving an equal amount of necessary food, instead of some getting numbers of parcels and others none at all. In one instance, a man, by dint of writing to every committee and organization, was receiving over a hundred parcels a month, thereby supporting two German families.

THE ARRIVAL OF THE PARCELS

That parcels meant a great deal to the prisoners is obvious from the fact that they are mentioned time and again.

Mr. J. Brassington, who was taken prisoner in March, 1918, says: 'The hunger was terrible, and living under the conditions we were, men's minds were getting deranged. We would pluck and eat the grass that grew under the barbed wire that surrounded the compound. I began to feel exhausted, used to dream of food all the time, the craving for it was terrible. . . .

'However, after four months' captivity my first Red Cross parcel arrived from England. This gave me new life and some encouragement to live—my prayer had been answered at last.'

Mr. P. E. Connor also refers to the parcels. He was at Neuhammer-am-Queis, not far distant from Breslau, which was a military training centre and contained a very large prisoner of war camp. '. . . On our arrival we were put into the hospital attached to the camp until such time as we were considered fit for work. The country all round us was very flat and all one could see was large stretches of sandy soil and pine forests. It was from here that we were first officially reported as being prisoners, our names being taken and forwarded through the Red Cross in Switzerland to the British Authorities. I afterwards discovered that I had been reported as "Missing" by the War Office, and the first intimation my parents received that I was still alive was a post card which I was able to send on arrival at this camp. The conditions here, compared with what we had previously experienced, were very good as we had quite good beds and clean clothes. The food rations were very scanty, but we received occasional issues of biscuits and tinned meat from the Red Cross in Switzerland which were very welcome. After a couple of weeks in hospital I was considered fit and was transferred to the ordinary camp. Here again the food was terrible and as far as possible we endeavoured to live on the contents of the Red Cross parcels received.' Mr. Connor was with the 12th Royal Irish Rifles when taken prisoner on 21st March, 1918. He was repatriated in January, 1919, and posted to the 1st Royal Irish Rifles.

Mr. R. P. Gubbins, who was wounded and captured in front of Arras, was sent to a tar-distilling factory in Duisberg, Rhineland, when he left hospital at Minden. His daily rations were two bowls of mangel-wurzel soup, two bowls of black coffee and a quarter of a loaf of black bread. He says : '. . . We fed on our parcels, which were excellent, sent from England and protected by the Neutral Governments.'

A SAUSAGE AT LILLE

Before leaving the subject of food we give one further extract from the experiences of Mr. R. Walbancke and Mr. W. S. Casserley. The story is a trivial one, but behind it lies the history of a friendship of two Prudential men whom the War threw together. Mr. Casserley tells the story.

'The night was wearing on and the two o'clock guard had been changed some minutes ; I usually waited to see this performance and viewed it as a kind of landmark in the night, signifying that it was about time for me to seek some sleep. There was a remarkable absence of ceremony about the affair ; one Jerry simply arrived with his rifle, and the other walked off ! No challenge or password, sometimes not even a grunt !

'On this occasion the new-comer had stood at his post at our end for a few moments, and then moved off down to the other end of the courtyard. All was quiet and no one in sight, and I was just turning away from the window when my ear caught the sound of someone coming down the tunnel which gave on to the courtyard. Had it been time for the guard to change there would have been nothing to attract my attention, but this was such an unusual event that I lingered at the bars to try to find out what was happening. The advancing footsteps rang out sharp and clear in the silence of the night, and the next moment a German soldier appeared at the tunnel entrance walking rapidly and with decision ; he turned half-right as he emerged into view, came straight across, without looking to either left or right, to the window at which I stood, placed something on the ledge in front of me, swung round on his heels without uttering a word and, marching back as he had come, disappeared into the tunnel again and the sound of his retreating steps quickly died away.

'It all happened so unexpectedly and found me so unprepared that for some seconds after he had gone I could only gaze in astonishment at the once more deserted courtyard. As in a dream I had instinctively caught up what he placed in front of me even as he put it there, and had hidden it in my pocket, but the action was altogether involuntary and I had no idea what I had acquired in such strange fashion. I soon collected my scattered senses, however, and looked round cautiously to see if anyone else had been a witness of the incident: but all was quiet behind me, no one stirred—evidently I was the only one awake. Then, very carefully, I withdrew my hand from my pocket, keeping it hidden from any chance observer in the cell and, standing with my back to everyone else there I slowly opened my hand, trembling with excitement the while. *Before my astonished gaze lay three inches of German sausage.*

'I could scarcely believe the evidence of my own eyes, and after a momentary hesitation raised the sausage to my nose for verification. Yes, there could be no mistake, it smelt like *meat*, and fresh meat, too. Surely two of my senses could not combine to deceive me? My mouth watered as I looked at it again: and then, in the dead of night and to all intents and purposes alone, I was assailed by the most powerful temptation I had ever encountered.

'It may seem absurd to maintain that the trial of a lifetime should centre round a small portion of sausage, but it must be remembered that this was the first piece of meat I had seen since our capture, and the privations of the last four days had reduced us all to a state where solid food was a subject that continually pervaded our thoughts and conversation. I had merely to eat what I held in my hand and no one would ever be any the wiser; furthermore it had been given to me for that express purpose. But there are some things that civilization simply will not let us do, let cynics say what they will, and collecting myself I made the necessary effort and once more placed my treasure in my pocket.

'Silently I moved over to where Wally slept and slightly shook his shoulder.

'"Wally," I whispered in his ear, and he started up.

'"Sh——" I continued in the same tone, "come and look here," and I turned and crept back to the window.

'Wally was beside me in an instant, the tone of my voice, low as it was, having conveyed to him a sense of something unusual.

'"What is it, Cass?" he murmured.

'For answer I again drew my hand from my pocket and opened it. He stared in amazement.

'" Sausage," he gasped at length, and quickly added : " Where-ever did you get it from ? "

'" Never mind," I replied. " Let's eat it quickly before anyone wakes."

'" Suppose it's poisoned," whispered Wally.

'" We shall soon know ! " I suggested.

'There was a short pause, then he asked :

'" How shall we divide it ? "

'" You take a bite, and then I'll take a bite," I breathed in his ear, and he nodded.

'So he nibbled a piece off and I followed suit : turn by turn we slowly demolished what was to us a miraculous gift that might well turn the scale in our favour in the trial through which we were passing. We made it last as long as we could in spite of the ravenous state we were in. Such a feast deserved to be dwelt upon ! '

ARMISTICE

In many cases the prisoners did not know for some time afterwards that the Armistice had been signed. Mr. G. J. Gould of the Queen's Westminster Rifles, who was taken by the Germans on 27th May, 1918, gives us the following interesting note :

'Most of my time as a prisoner was spent at a coal-mine near Zeitz in Saxony, where our living quarters were a few yards from the pit-head. Of the seventy or so prisoners forming this " Commando " twelve were British, the remainder being Russian, French and Italian. We were not allowed newspapers and as the few letters we received were censored, we were entirely without news of the progress of the war.

'Naturally, we were not enthusiastic workers, but attempts at malingering, while frequent, were seldom successful. During November, 1918, however, it was noticed that prisoners reporting themselves as unfit were all being excused work. In a very short time all the British were on the sick-list.

'When we were told that on resuming duty at the mine we should be granted a substantial increase in our weekly pay of 4·88 marks (the most that mine ever bought was three small apples), we began to suspect that the end of the War was near. The inducement of a rise did not have the desired effect and some time afterwards we were moved to another "Commando". In villages through which we passed, banners bearing inscriptions such as "Welcome Home to our Victorious Soldiers" caused us some bewilderment, and it was with considerable relief that we later learned the terms of the Armistice which had been signed several weeks previously.'

Mr. W. Allan, whose earlier experiences we have recounted, tells of another prison camp experience. He was at Limburg-an-Lahn camp at the time of the Armistice, when the German soldiers, aided by townspeople, rioted and chased every officer out of the camp. Discontent had long been brewing. There was a state of tension as to what might happen. To ward off the danger of an invasion of the camp by the mob, the German under-officers requested the co-operation of the British and French prisoners in preserving the peace and even offered to arm them if necessary.

We give a further quotation from the pen of Mr. W. S. Casserley as a final picture. This was at the prisoners of war camp at Parchim.

'Then came the great day, the ninth of November, when we awoke to find a red flag flying above every Jerry guard-house, and to be confronted with smiling Postens and Feldwebels, who informed us that the Army had revolted, that there had been a revolution (practically bloodless, so well and secretly had it been organized), that the Kaiser had been forced to abdicate and had fled to Holland, and, finally, that the Armistice would be signed within forty-eight hours, this being the object of the revolution. To all in the Allied countries who look back on these stirring times Armistice Day is the landmark, but, to those in Germany, Revolution Day marked the acme of the excitement; the country was swept by a wave of intense relief that penetrated even the seclusion of the Lager, and thrilled every man in it. We knew that the signing of the Armistice would follow automatically; we knew, too, that our side had won and that we should soon be home once more.

'The Germans told us that everything would be arranged as speedily as possible and that, in the meantime, we must carry on just as usual. We quite saw the force of this point of view and agreed to do as requested, with one important reservation: the War was over and our side was victorious, so, although we were willing to keep within the camp, no Englishman would do any more work.'

These and many other Prudential men suffered in the hands

of the enemy. The following names are of those whose stories we have been unable to include :

F. Bagshaw	R. M. Jones	J. B. H. Roberts
H. M. Binsted	C. S. Judd	W. J. Robertson
A. H. Boxwell	W. A. Leach	P. Rocker
T. A. Brangwin	P. Liversedge	P. F. G. Sayer
C. H. Bright	J. F. Mance	P. W. Shelley
C. Brockway	J. Matthews	H. Smith
G. H. Burnip	J. McCall	R. S. Standfield
A. Chapman	P. McDonald	J. M. Stewart
W. H. Chasty	A. S. Minns	F. W. E. Symonds
S. W. Dunthorne	G. Moore	S. G. Thompson
C. A. Earthy	H. Morris	C. Thomson
H. F. Ford	C. Mortimer	R. A. Turnbull
A. E. Geeson	J. R. Munday	T. W. Watts
A. H. Harding	T. Orrell	F. C. Welch
D. Harley	W. Pawson	H. A. White
J. Hembling	F. J. Phipps	H. P. White
J. Hercock	G. A. Rain	F. L. Williams
G. J. Isaacs	K. E. Redway	J. H. Wright
F. Izod	E. E. Rivett	

MISSING DEATH BY INCHES

THERE are men now in the service of the Company who had miraculous escapes from death in the War.

Mr. A. D. Bayliss was leaving Poperinghe on the 22nd December, 1917, with guns and ammunition for Bully-Grenay. The Germans were shelling heavily. A piece of shrapnel pierced the lorry in which Mr. Bayliss was sitting, shattering a haversack which hung close to him. The shrapnel skimmed his face, causing the blood to flow, but otherwise he was unhurt. The haversack was blown to pieces.

At night, whilst one of a party marching in file on the parados of a trench in the Vimy Sector, Mr. W. E. Beagley felt a slight tug on his tunic pocket. Later he found that the button on his pocket had been struck, the bullet entering the pocket and coming out at the back of the tunic.

Mr. J. E. Butler had a charmed life. Four men each side of him were blown up and he stood unhurt. On the same day a sniper caught six men and one officer who were all round him and again he escaped. Then he was twice buried up to the neck and still unharmed.

Mr. C. W. Cutter was one of those who believed that he received some kind of mysterious inner warning of danger. He was detailed to sweep down a private house from top to bottom by an officer to whom he was acting as batman. He could have completed his task in another ten minutes but received what he calls a 'silent message' warning him of danger. He did not stay to finish and had not walked more than twenty-five yards from the building when a shell wrecked it completely.

In the offensive of 27th May, 1918, Mr. W. F. Elsy was the only Non-Commissioned Officer left in his regiment. All the Officers and other N.C.O.s had been killed and there were only 60 men left.

When in Serbia Mr. F. W. Foster was sitting with a comrade near a fire. Neither of them wished to leave it to secure a supper but eventually Mr. Foster agreed to go. Immediately after he left his friend was blown to pieces. The fire had been lighted over a buried live shell.

Mr. W. B. Laverock was being transported from one position to another in a covered motor lorry when a shell burst, the splinters flying through the cover, killing the men on either side of him but missing him completely.

Mr. H. H. R. Vann owes his life to the fact that he went to speak to another Prudential man. The incident happened in France towards the end of October, 1917. Vann was sent away from his Ambulance suffering from an attack of trench fever and found himself at a Casualty Clearing Station run by the First City of London R.A.M.C. He knew that a number of Prudential men were serving in this unit. After he had been in the casualty clearing station—a group of canvas marquees—for about two days he was allowed to get up. He walked to the other end of the line of marquees to see if he could find a Prudential colleague. He did so and stood talking to him. Then a German aeroplane dropped five bombs in succession across the row of marquees. One of the bombs dropped on Vann's bed. The casualties were thirty killed and seventy wounded. This was a German reprisal for an alleged attack on a German hospital train.

Mr. R. H. Welch was once stranded in the bush in German East Africa with a motor lorry for fourteen days with only three days' rations of biscuits. He was found half dead by an officer and taken to hospital. Fourteen days later he was believed to be actually dead and was taken to the mortuary. Next day, however, he was found to be alive and was taken back to the hospital.

Mr. P. H. E. Wood's life was once saved by his Bible, which was cut through up to the 23rd Chapter of the Acts of the Apostles. He still has the Bible in his possession.

Mr. F. C. Kirby had an extraordinary escape near Ostend. In March, 1917, whilst bombing German destroyers off Zeebrugge, his aeroplane lost formation owing to a cloud and became separated from the flight. Near Ostend a German scout positioned himself on the tail of Kirby's aeroplane. Bullets pierced the petrol-tanks and Kirby was wounded in the lung. His machine nose-dived vertically and the crew of four were thrown into the sea. It was decided that two should attempt to swim to shore, which was about two miles distant. They were never heard of again. The third stayed with Kirby and cut off his leather coat and top boots, which were dragging him down. Presently a British machine approached flying high, but was driven off by anti-aircraft fire. After a further long wait two French flying-boats approached. The first to alight had engine and top plane blown away by the land guns. The pilot, observer and gunner were taken prisoners. The observer of the second pulled Kirby aboard as the machine taxied on the sea and he arrived at Dunkirk after a trip in severe weather clad only in a vest. The pilot, a probationary officer, had been forbidden to attempt the rescue. He was court-martialled, promoted Lieutenant on the spot, awarded the Legion of Honour, and the D.S.O. by the British Government.

Mr. A. H. Hagon's life was saved by a horse. He was sent with an important message to a Battery Commander. Although he knew the direction he soon became lost owing to general obstacles. His horse suddenly stopped and would not proceed. Dismounting he made the usual examination of the hooves for stones. Mounting again he urged the horse on but with no success. Down jumped Mr. Hagon and tugged the reins, but still the horse would not budge. At length our colleague gave it up, and once more mounting let the horse do as he wanted. The beast turned to the right but after a short distance allowed Mr. Hagon once more to guide him in the direction he wanted to go. The message was delivered and Mr. Hagon returned without anything unusual happening. The next day he walked to where this incident happened and discovered a ' tank trap ' with probably 5 or 6 feet of water in the pit, the whole being camouflaged with wire-netting and green material. Had the horse gone a few steps forward Mr. Hagon would not have lived to tell the story.

Mr. G. H. Gilbert was wounded by a piece of shell casing. This piece, which was about one inch in diameter, entered the thigh close to the groin and, splitting in two almost immediately, passed clean through the leg in right-angled directions. One of the doctors who examined him said he had had a remarkably fortunate escape as one or other of the pieces should have severed the femoral artery, in which case he would have bled to death in about a minute, failing which one or other piece should have hit the bone, which would have meant the loss of his leg.

Mr. H. J. Young, whose experiences are given on page 98, owes his life to the excellent shooting of a German sniper. This sniper had caused great individual losses to the unit. Mr. Young was visiting a shell hole post in which were a Platoon Sergeant and four men. He was talking to the Sergeant when the sniper fired. Mr. Young and the Sergeant offered a large target and as usual the sniper got the centre, but that centre in this case was the small space between the two men.

INCIDENTS

Mr. A. T. Burton was on the way home commanding a train from Marseilles with two other officers and 300 troops. At Lyons the train stopped and Mr. Burton and a brother officer in their pyjamas (it was 8 a.m.) crossed the rails to go to the refreshment room. When they returned the train had gone. They travelled to Paris in pyjamas and arrived at midnight.

Mr. A. H. Flintham, when wounded, came home on the hospital ship *Kalyon* from Havre to Southampton. He had to wait two nights in Havre because submarines were in the Channel. He paid twenty francs to an orderly to get him to a London hospital, but when he woke next morning he found he was in Aberdeen.

Mr. J. Hall tells of this incident which occurred behind the line in the Ypres Salient. 'All the Company were roused about 1 a.m. and told to get on parade as every man must go into the line at once. It was pitch dark and the officers experienced some difficulty in getting the men into order. Whilst this was going on someone shouted "Get your Prudential policies ready and let Jos (Mr. Hall) mark them before we go in".' Mr. Hall had, a few days previous to this, received a box of chocolates from the office and his friends found out whence they had come.

In order to avoid the Boy Scout appearance of his Trench Mortar Battery on the march with their hand-cart, Mr. C. V. F. Manning 'acquired' a handy two-wheeled French farm-cart with horse and complete harness. This cart proved invaluable for carrying guns, base plates, personal equipment and rifles on the march, and once or twice was brought into service for carrying T.M. Ammunition into the line when the usual infantry carrying party could not be obtained. One night on the Somme orders had been given for a certain amount of ammunition to be in each gun-pit before daybreak, but men could not be spared to carry it in. Consequently the horse and cart were brought into the scheme. Every precaution was taken to prevent noise; the horses' hooves were wrapped in sandbags, the harness swathed in rags and the wheels well greased. Moreover, the cart was festooned with branches of trees and branches were carried by the men in case a Véry light exposed them. All went well until the last load arrived at the gun-pit, when a Véry light went up and the whole group froze with their branches sticking upward like a Christmas tree screen in front of the horse and cart. Everyone thought they would be blown to pieces in the next second, but flimsy though the camouflage was, it answered, and nobody was touched. Needless to say no time was lost in unloading when the light had faded out, nor in retiring without noise to a more sheltered spot where a deep breath could be taken.

Mr. J. Methven took part in the offensive in Italy in the autumn of 1918, when large numbers of Austrian Cavalry surrendered to our forces. A Company Captain and Lieutenant of the Gordon Highlanders coveted the handsome chargers and could not resist commandeering one each until rations would not permit retention any longer. Mr. Methven and another Gordon Highlander were ordered to get rid of the horses, but having cared for them for about a week they thought of turning them over for some gain. They exchanged them for two hens and two rabbits and had a square meal.

A sidelight on military censorship: Mr. F. C. W. Prosser saw His Late Majesty King George V at Reninghelst, Belgium, and wrote a descriptive letter to his wife regarding this incident. After the letter had been censored all she could read was 'Your loving husband, F.'

Mr. H. P. G. Roberts's first crossing to Ireland was an experience he will always remember. Five hundred men and five hundred bicycles (they were a Cyclist Regiment then) were compelled to keep below decks owing to the very rough sea and submarine menace. As the boat had been previously used for cattle transport and had not been cleaned out conditions were terrible. The bicycles broke loose owing to the rough sea. When finally the men landed at Dublin they were greeted with a shower of bricks from the inhabitants.

In September, 1917, Mr. T. Salter went over the top at Langemark, the object being to capture a German 'pill-box'. Having attained the objective the men got into the 'pill-box'. They had not been inside five minutes before one of them startled the others by saying that the pin had come out of his Mills bomb. Every man tried to get out at once and some stuck. Eventually there were three left. They told the man to hold his pocket whilst they cut it out. When this had been done it was discovered that the Mills bomb was only a box of matches which had fused.

When near Ham, Mr. A. P. Turner made a vegetable garden in front of his office. The General, when visiting the camp, was pleased with the idea and requested him to arrange for vegetables to be grown in all the available spaces. A few weeks afterwards German shells destroyed the whole work.

Mr. W. Wallace whilst on the way through the province of Azerbaijan in South Russia passed with a body of troops through a narrow gorge which took the best part of two days to negotiate. Suddenly they were confronted with a pile of huge boulders strewn across the roadway, barring their passage. They got in touch with the officer in charge of a fort which was situated on top of a very high cliff and after examination of the passport the Captain and his unit were allowed to proceed. They had covered about a kilometre when they were again stopped. This time it was an Armenian officer, and to their surprise they discovered that a battle had been stopped especially to allow the unit to pass through.

A private in Mr. S. E. J. Woods's section had a glass eye. He was in the habit of putting this eye near his ration of bread and instructing it to look after the bread whilst he washed. One of his comrades being hungry, stole the bread and also the eye. As a result the following appeared in Battalion Orders :

'The Commanding Officer fully appreciates the humour caused by the loss of Private Hartley's eye, but insists that the eye be returned within twelve hours or disciplinary action will be taken.'

COINCIDENCES

Mr. J. Mills was, for a time, at Blackpool. The men were billeted in houses for the winter, and he was detailed to pay out the billet money to the householders. The Battery Office was in the house in which he was born in 1877.

Mr. H. E. Taylor had a colleague in the same tent sleeping next to him with the same surname, initials and birthday.

Mr. W. J. Treleaven was one of thirteen survivors of a company of the Royal Warwickshire Regiment which took part in the attack on Oppy Wood. He was returning to rest when to his astonishment he saw his brother, who was in the Royal Field Artillery, and having heard Mr. Treleaven's Battalion was in the line had looked him up. The company rested for four days and was about to return to the line when to Mr. Treleaven's surprise he met his brother again with another brother who had originally been drafted to the Dardanelles.

Mr. W. S. Casserley, when a prisoner of war, talked to a German soldier who spoke perfect English. It transpired that this German soldier had lived in London for some years and had travelled regularly on Mr. Casserley's usual train up to Town in the morning.

THE DUKE OF WINDSOR

Mr. G. R. Aucutt tells this interesting story: 'At the end of September, 1916, my Battery was ordered up to one of the ridges between Morval and Les Bœufs (Somme). The situation was obscure and open, as our infantry had only just advanced. Enemy shelling was almost continuous and casualties were heavy. In October a Senior Staff Officer arrived one morning with the Prince of Wales, the former to interview our Major. I had some fifteen minutes' conversation with the Prince, who was interested in details of our life from day to day. Exactly twenty-four hours after the Prince had left us, the Battery was viciously shelled, the exact line having been "given away" by an enemy aeroplane. Six of our men were killed. *The shell fell precisely where the Prince and the Officer stood at the same hour on the day before.*'

On the 13th April, 1915, Mr. E. S. Cooper enlisted as a Bugler in the Royal Naval Division. In June of the same year he became an Able Seaman. Later he served as a Sub-Lieutenant in the Royal Naval Volunteer Reserve. In 1918 he returned from France and trained as a Pilot with the Royal Air Force at Reading, but owing to the Armistice he had to rejoin the Royal Naval Division at Alnwick in February, 1919. Before serving in France Mr. Cooper was in Gallipoli. In March, 1921, Mr. Cooper rejoined the Royal Naval Volunteer Reserve, which he represented on board H.M.S. *Renown* on its world tour with the Prince of Wales, the Company granting him leave.

Mr. E. A. H. Goldfinch tells us: 'One of the officers of my Battalion of the Grenadier Guards was the Prince of Wales, whom I frequently saw in and out of the trenches, mud-bespattered as any ordinary 2nd Lieutenant.'

Mr. W. L. Sadler conducted a party, of which the Prince of Wales was a member, over Kemmel Hill in December, 1915, and Mr. C. J. E. Daily talked to the Prince, not knowing his identity until told later by the O.C.

GALLIPOLI

At daybreak on April 25th, 1915, General Sir Ian Hamilton began his attack on the Gallipoli Peninsula. Sir Ian's plan comprised two main converging attacks on the southern end of the Peninsula. The first was to be by the 29th Division at five separate simultaneous landings in the vicinity of Cape Helles, and the second by the Australian and New Zealand Army Corps near Gaba Tepe. At a point known as 'V' Beach, over 2,000 men of the Dublin and Munster Fusiliers and the Hampshire Regiment were packed in the hold of the *River Clyde*, a steamer specially prepared for landing troops, and were carried to within a few yards of the shore. At the same time the rest of the Dublin Fusiliers approached the shore in boats. Annihilating fire burst on them from all parts. The boats and the edge of the beach were heaped with dead and dying. Terrible firing also took place on 'W' Beach. Here the Lancashire Fusiliers were towed and rowed to the shore in thirty or forty cutters. Undeterred by the most severe losses the men waded from the water and with marvellous discipline actually reformed their lines along the beach.

When the day ended lodgment had been effected upon all the five beaches attacked and about 9,000 men had been disembarked, but of these at least 3,000 were killed or wounded and the remainder were clinging precariously to their dearly bought footholds around the rim of the Peninsula.

The glorious and tragic drama of the Gallipoli Peninsula, including the Battle of Suvla Bay, which Churchill describes as the most heart-breaking episode in the annals of the British Army, was enacted throughout the remainder of the year 1915. The Peninsula was evacuated at the end of the year, yet here might have been an outstanding victory which would almost certainly have shortened the period of the War.

THE DETAILED TRUTH

Here is a letter written on 3rd September, 1915, from Alexandria by Mr. A. H. Wild. It presents a vivid picture of high spirits and courage in the face of fearful conditions.

'Looking back on Egypt is like dreaming about "Paradise Lost", it certainly was fearfully hot, and flies were an abomination, but compared to this—well, words fail me.

'Egypt, the land of comparative peace and quiet, our splendidly conditioned horses, bright swords and other gear, smart drill uniforms, afternoon sleeps. "Gallipoli"—and this is honest truth—footing it, packs on our backs, what is left of them, one shirt, three weeks' dirt on it, one pair of socks all holes, no soap, no towels, not even a tooth-brush, just a pick and shovel, a rifle and bayonet, 400 rounds of ammunition, and if you are lucky an overcoat. And we have only had these for a few days. We are shelled morning, noon and evening and sniped at all the whole night through. You cook your own food when you can get wood, when you can't you live on "bully", biscuits and water. Water is our great trouble here, and we have lost nearly an army getting water, such as it is. So, do we waste it washing? No, thanks! It is now twenty days since I had a wash or shave. (A shell has just cracked the parapet in front of our "dug-out", not six feet away, and turned my cloak inside out.) We have all got beards (two more shells have burst over the trench whilst writing this short passage) and about one-third of the old crowd are either killed, wounded, missing or sick.

'Of the Ibis men who came with us three are *hors de combat.* Duffin, so often reported killed, was, I am sorry to say, twice wounded by shrapnel in an advance from the landing-place, and I fear Dulieu is seriously hurt. He was shot in the chest and had to be left to the stretcher-bearers who came over the ground later on, and nothing has since been heard of him.

'"Jimmy" Taylor retired from the trenches last night on the sick list, leaving Ledgard,[1] Moate,[2] Pulsford [3] and myself to "carry on" for the "Ibis". Apropos Dulieu,[4] our one and only motto

[1] G. F. Ledgard served throughout the War. He was in camp with the Yeomanry when war was declared and was with the Army of Occupation in Germany in 1919. He served in Egypt, Sinai Desert, Suez Canal Zone and the Western Front. He was in the Suvla Bay landing.

[2] C. G. W. Moate was a Trooper in the Middlesex Yeomanry when war was declared. He was at Suvla Bay in August, 1915, and subsequently invalided home. From April, 1916 to March, 1917, he was in Ireland and from March to June, 1917, at the Cadet School at Bisley. In December, 1917, he went to France with the Tank Corps.

[3] L. M. Pulsford was also in the Yeomanry when war was declared. He served in Egypt, Salonica and Palestine and was demobilized in February, 1919. A letter from Pulsford will be found on page 140 written from a hospital in Southport.

[4] L. G. Dulieu was killed on 21st August, 1915, while engaged on stretcher-bearing under heavy fire.

in such cases, and very strictly adhered to also, is " presume the best ". Therefore I am pleased to say there is every possibility that he may have been picked up and put on board a hospital ship ; if so there would be no possibility of us hearing from him yet. And if it is of any comfort to his people, I may add that all identity discs and other property of fallen men come to me personally, and I have not had his, or any report or rumour of his death. On the brighter side also, " shot in the chest ", is something that sounds bad, but since being in this " hell ", I have seen men shot right through the chest and walking back to the hospital unaided, and *smoking* !

'Possibly many of your readers will have heard of the advance of the 2nd Mounted Division over three miles or so of open country under a fiendish hail of shrapnel, and the attack on the Turkish positions after a rest of twenty minutes only. Perhaps it has not been reported in detail, *nor the losses* ; perhaps the truth will come out later ; let's hope so. But in any case I feel that I can say, without fear of being boastful, that the old Regiment, and likewise the whole Division, was magnificent.

'I can speak best of course for the Regiment, as I was in front with the Acting Adjutant (Mr. Wedgwood Benn), and when the trial came I am afraid I expected a stampede in all directions, for it was our first experience of bad shelling over absolutely open ground ; instead of which I looked round and saw them marching along like a regiment on parade in London, and the order to double was given only during the last three or four hundred yards, and then they still kept perfect order. Just behind me was an officer leading his troop quietly on, one bullet still in his foot and another in his face. I had an awful load of stuff, and looked like Pickford's, and he laughed at me as far as he was able.

'I saw another shell burst right over Duffin and the troop behind him, and down went eight of my old troop together, all old pals of mine, Duffin with them.

'My personal feelings were so peculiar that I cannot now analyse them, but something seemed to keep saying, " Get on with it ", so I got on with it until a shell came and separated " Headquarters " although no one was hurt. I lost the Adjutant and was wondering whether it was worth while trying to carry in a dead man whom I fell over (funny things one does think about in such cases), when another shell came plonk right on me, and said, " Get on with it ", so I put on top gear and just reached our first " collecting spot " and fell behind a bank as a shell emptied the whole bag of tricks over me. I had still about 150 yards to go, but only rifle-fire this time, and although it sounds absurd it was a positive relief after the shelling, and I quite enjoyed the final walk. On looking back from a safe spot I found that great patches of the ground behind us were on fire.

'It was chiefly here that Mr. Aucutt's son-in-law, Shepherd, proved himself such a hero. He is a stretcher-bearer, and with his comrades they did V.C.s work in and out of that burning slaughter-house, which was still under shell-fire. Dulieu was a stretcher-bearer also, and I believe he went down whilst engaged in the same work. Were I to write quires I could never do justice to the heroic deeds done by the " Medical Staff " on that day, particularly by the stretcher-bearers.

'To continue : the Regiment (and likewise the Division) was reformed, and we went forward to the attack—to give a detailed account of which would be to invoke the wrath of the Censor and get this epistle torn up, so I am afraid I must return to the " ego ", as it is best to speak of one's own experience. Well, we doubled round our protective hill and at once came under rifle-fire, and from that moment my memory only serves me so far as to bring back to mind a series of endless rushes from cover to cover, with so many narrow escapes and incidents that it is impossible to give a clear description, except perhaps to say that through all this the " boys " were perfectly cool and in hand, as one incident will show. We were racing across some shingly ground, when a bullet hit some stones in front and something caught me on the knee. I turned a complete somersault and thought I was done. Someone coming behind remarked, " Hallo ! Wild. Did you fall or were you pushed ? " . . . What I said does not matter.

'We reached some advanced trenches and waited for the Turks to be driven into the open—it was intended that we should get them with the bayonet. As for the " driving party " on our left—well, there are still over 200 graves and they are not all buried yet. From the trenches where we were three days ago, I could plainly see the " scene " of that " affair ", a field of equipment and ugly contorted heaps, with here and there the blue uniform of a Turk, and at night when it was dark the smell came down to us. That was the 21st August. This is 3rd September, and we are still in the trenches, although we have moved to another part, thank God ! But I understand they are not all buried yet—too many snipers about.

'I wonder if the truth about Gallipoli will ever come out. If it does, your readers will understand what a lot might have been put in a letter of this description were it not for fear of censorship.

'" Between the lines " is a hackneyed phrase, but no one can possibly read sufficiently " between the lines " of our newspaper reports to get the slightest idea of what has and still goes on here. Men here who have been in France, say that the " game " there is a pastime to the conditions here. We found two dead men down our main well yesterday.

'And are we downhearted? Certainly not! and we are out for a win if a win depends on fortitude and pluck. I did not believe such men existed as I see on all sides every day, but it is a hard job, and they are very tired and reduced in numbers.

'If the detailed truth of this picnic is ever told, it will astonish even England.'

A prophetic utterance!

IN THE TRENCHES AT GALLIPOLI

A first-hand description of the conditions after our men had established themselves on the Peninsula, written from a hospital in Chatham on February 16th, 1916, by Mr. A. R. Peters.

'We were landed at midnight on " W " Beach, beside the famous *River Clyde*. Our first impressions of Turkey were not at all favourable, insomuch as we had a choking, dusty, two-mile march, or rather stagger, across what seemed to be deep fine sand to the camp. It afterwards appeared that the reliable Indian guide had lost his way, which drew forth " curses, not loud but deep ". In due course we were put in our companies and sections (as we were reinforcements), and proceeded to occupy our respective " dug-outs ". The camp routine, as far as fatigues, meals, etc., was much the same as at home, but of course there was no squad drill or field operations. We were favoured with considerable attention from " Asiatic Annie ", a gun which had a nasty habit of disappearing after each shot, thus rendering our fire rather futile.

'The country around was arid, extremely dusty and dry, with scanty vegetation. Still we had some very welcome sea-bathing on " W " Beach. It was a grand time in the cool water after the heat of the land.

'First time in the trenches was not without some misgivings, but these were soon overcome by the novelty of the thing. After a long tramp of about five miles over land laid waste everywhere and long and tortuous communication trenches, we eventually arrived at, first the reserve trenches, then the " supports " and lastly the firing line.

In Gallipoli, at Cape Helles at any rate, a great many of the British trenches were really old Turkish ones, abandoned by the Turks after the first small advances. These were hardly the model of the latest trench construction, but they provided plenty of rough shelters " dug under " the sides. During the " prickly " heat of the summer the trenches were intolerable. Everyone quickly assumed the copper tint. There was no way of escaping from the sun. Culinary operations had reached the stage of a fine art, especially when apricot jam was turned into a desirable " chutney " for the officers. Night was the worst time in the trenches. In the firing line, after " stand-to-arms " at dusk, one had to keep watch every hour and get what rest was possible in the intervening hours. When in the supports and reserves, working parties of all descriptions are necessary. The pick and shovel came into constant use. It is rather peculiar when a London clerk has to go underground with a little pick and hack away at an earthy ceiling in pitch darkness. However, these incidents are rather enjoyed owing to their very absurdity.

'Winter in the trenches is altogether different. They are converted into canals, so the introduction of a " trench-boat " would be welcome. The nights, too, are so long, that to keep awake in the last watches in the early morning is really hard work. When the water does subside, it leaves behind the stickiest mud in creation, the like of which is never seen in England. It rains in these regions—at least from the brief experience we had—in a series of heavy showers. Sometimes there will be one terrific downpour, and then it will be quite clear and calm again. One night this happened while we were in the Rest Camp ; it poured for about an hour just after sunset. Everyone was washed out of their dug-outs and had to stand shivering, looking at their flooded homes. The moon came out after the storm and the night was grand. The only sound was the sea, not yet calmed down after being lashed into fury. Towards the end of the Gallipolian occupation the Turks made a great increase in guns and shells. However, the French replied (as also did we ourselves) vigorously with their wonderful " 75's " and aerial torpedoes. These latter sail over to the enemy trenches, one can see them in the air, and explode with terrific concussion, sending up huge volumes of smoke.

'My turn came at last to get wounded by a bomb. I was quickly moved away from the line, and after a series of short journeys from different ambulance stations, I eventually found myself in a bed on a hospital ship, which conveyed me to Malta. It was good to have a nice bed, good food, and to be away from shell-fire for a bit. From Malta I was sent to Devonport, and thence to Chatham by hospital train.'

WRITTEN IN A DUG-OUT

An extract from a letter written by Mr. P. D. Power at about the same period:

'. . . You will be interested to hear that this letter is being written in a dug-out on the side of a cliff-like hill on the Gallipoli Peninsula. The outlook is seawards, and over the horizon can be seen the tops of two mountainous islands. Signs and sounds of war are, of course, everywhere—the flash and whang of naval guns being among the more pleasant of these, and it is enormously comforting to reflect that the Navy is on our side and holds the sea. There are other sounds not so sweet, such as the whine of the shells, which the Turks know pretty accurately how to send into our depot here, and really there is not always time to get out of the scenery into the nearest dug-out before they burst their shower of shrapnel around.'

SUVLA BAY

A letter from Mr. L. M. Pulsford, written from a hospital at Southport:

'. . . It was early last April when the whole of the 2nd Mounted Division—to which our regiment belongs—left Avonmouth for Egypt, where but for one mishap it arrived some ten days later. One of the transports, which had the horses on board, was torpedoed after leaving the Bristol Channel. Luckily the boat managed to reach harbour in safety, and no lives were lost. Perfect weather attended us on the voyage out, which was full of interest to me. Arriving in Egypt the Division was split up and the various Brigades distributed about the country. For a week our Brigade was encamped on the seashore a few miles from Alexandria. As you may guess, it was not a very pleasant week for us, unused as we were to the intense heat; in fact it was a week of sickness for nearly all of us. At the end of the week we shifted down to Ismailia, which is situated on Lake Timshah, mid-way between Suez and Port Said. We were encamped about a mile outside the town (which although small, was a delightful relief from the desert which surrounded us). There were also several regiments of Indian Cavalry and Infantry stationed with us. Four months slipped away, during which time we continued our training as cavalry, at the same time acting as part of the defensive force for the Canal. Some weeks before we got to Egypt an attempt was made to cross the Suez Canal, but it proved an utter failure. Nothing happened, however, during our sojourn there, although I don't think the Turks have wholly abandoned the idea of another attack.

'It was early in August when we left for Gallipoli, and I don't think anything could have pleased us more! To a certain extent I knew what to expect, and I can assure you that things more than came up to my expectations. We landed at Suvla Bay, where, a few days before, a fresh landing had been made. We first came under fire on August 21st; it was a day to be remembered. No doubt you have read of the general attack that was unsuccessfully made on this occasion by the troops at Suvla Bay—including the Yeomanry Division. One of our Brigades actually succeeded in driving the Turks off Hill 70, suffering terrible losses in so doing, but by daybreak we had lost it again. I believe that so far we have not re-taken this hill. This was the only advance attempted during my time on the Peninsula. The Turks seemed content to remain in their trenches, and we, for obvious reasons, in ours. Our position in the Suvla Bay region was none too strong, and before anything could be done it was necessary to strengthen our hold. When I left the place was a maze of trenches, zigzagging about the country. My experience of war is that nine-tenths of the time is spent in preparing trenches, strengthening and guarding them, and one-tenth in actual fighting. It is hard work from morning till night—nothing but guards and fatigues. For five weeks I had only one complete night's rest, and that was because I was feeling queer. The whole night long the digging continues, and if you are not digging you are generally on guard.

'The work, strenuous though it was, would have seemed easier to us if we had had decent food. I believe that a lot of the dysentery may be attributed to the lack of fresh food, such as bread and meat. Both of these foodstuffs were scarce, and when we did get them they were almost unfit for consumption. Drinking water, as you know, has proved a source of difficulty, and in some parts of the Peninsula it is so scarce that it has been necessary to import it; hundreds of cans containing water are sent daily from Alexandria.

'I need not say anything about the flies—they were simply terrible. It was under these conditions that I contracted dysentery, and was consequently sent away to Alexandria. I was in hospital there for four weeks, and then they told me I was being sent back to England.'

EVACUATION OF THE PENINSULA

'The evacuation left a great impression on my mind', writes Mr. N. Todd, 'as we could have been annihilated while on the beach waiting to embark, but no shot was fired by the Turks . . .'

Mr. E. Powell was evacuated on the 9th January, 1916, being one of the last twenty men to leave.

Mr. A. R. Peters states: '. . . The evacuation followed, carried out with such supreme efficiency that it made some amends for the tragedy of the Dardanelles.'

Mr. B. Gardner remained three days after the evacuation, having volunteered to remain to set mines and traps.

Of the Prudential men who took part in the Gallipoli Campaign and who are alive to-day we have been able to trace, in addition to those already mentioned, the following:

W. R. Adkins
S. Bandy
A. W. Beer
P. A. H. Bignell
R. M. Blackett
J. F. Browne
T. W. Butler
E. W. Carless
R. H. Copeman
F. H. Coppard
A. W. Cowper
J. Crossley
G. G. E. Daviss
A. Dew
E. C. Filby
J. B. Garwood
A. F. Gleed
A. W. Green
S. J. Gurnett
W. C. Hogge
B. W. Horton
H. Howden
F. C. Hughes
R. Lucas
R. McWilliams
W. Metcalf
H. E. Miller
F. Minney
W. G. Newby
H. J. Ockelford
P. J. O'Kelly
H. E. Parker
E. F. Patton
A. C. Prettyman
A. J. Rawlins
D. T. G. Ray
W. L. Rees
A. D. Strachan
R. A. R. Tamblin
H. Taylor
F. J. Ward
B. W. Webb
H. P. White
A. H. Windsor
H. Wingate
T. Woodward
J. Worthington
A. J. Wright

OTHER FRONTS

SALONICA

When the Austrians defeated the Serbs in 1915 the latter retreated towards Greece followed by the Bulgarian Army. Owing to the failure of the Greeks to abide by their treaty with Serbia it was feared the Bulgarians would overrun Macedonia and deprive the Allies of the use of the port of Salonica. This would have enabled Germany to establish a submarine base there and sever our Mediterranean communications. British and French troops were dispatched to Salonica and between 1915 and 1918 a great number of our men found themselves in Macedonia. Amongst those who had this experience were :

J. W. Akrill
C. A. Aldridge
A. W. Alexander
F. G. Arnold
H. J. G. Back
J. H. Balchin
J. Banks
P. Barratt
A. V. Beechener
V. E. Beeston
A. E. Bell
A. J. Booker
J. Bootland
W. F. Boston
H. Bourne
H. J. Bradley
S. A. Bramwell
P. H. Bridge
W. A. Bromley
J. T. Brookes
J. F. Browne
E. Burns
T. W. Butler
J. A. Buxton
C. J. Cable
F. A. Cobb
T. W. Collins
F. Cook
W. T. Cordell
E. Cornes
J. Cottis
A. W. Cowper
A. Cripps
G. G. Crowe
G. H. Davies
G. E. Daviss
V. M. Deakins
H. J. N. Debenham
A. Dew
L. A. Duckett
E. Duvall
A. S. R. Ellis
L. Ellis
R. B. Etherington
T. C. Farley
W. H. Farndale
J. R. Farrant
C. R. Farrell
S. Fazey
J. Felstead
D. C. Field
E. C. Filby
R. C. Foster
E. W. Freeman
L. W. Funston
A. F. Gale
P. C. Garratt
H. Golding
F. W. Gordon
T. W. Gowlett
A. W. Green
W. Guiver
S. J. Gurnett
J. Hardisty
L. P. C. Harvey
C. J. Hedger

M. T. Hingston
A. L. Hitchin
J. E. Holden
J. B. Hollis
B. C. Hoskins
C. A. Hubbard
F. C. Hughes
F. Izod
G. Jack
H. Jackson
D. Keir
A. S. King
G. H. Knowles
H. S. Lane
G. L. Latham
A. E. Lavers
G. F. Ledgard
H. C. Levett
F. V. H. Lewis
F. W. Lewis
W. B. Lewis
F. H. Lightfoot
L. Lindley
W. E. Lister
A. B. Maclean
W. O. Makinson
F. C. Manning
L. Mansfield
P. Martin
C. Miller
F. W. Morgan
W. H. Morrey
A. W. E. Morris
H. J. Ockelford
F. W. Ockwell
P. J. O'Kelly
F. W. G. Osborne
C. T. Outten
S. Owen
H. E. T. Palfreman
J. B. Patterson
E. F. Patton
R. A. Pedler
W. C. Phelp
H. Phillips
W. I. Pickard
C. Porter
C. H. D. Pratt
P. C. Prior
L. M. Pulsford
A. Reid
H. L. Richardson
J. W. Ridley
A. Risby
J. Ritchie
G. E. Robinson
W. Russell
F. S. Salter
H. W. Sayers
R. C. Shearlaw
W. A. Sherratt
W. H. Shufflebotham
A. J. Simmonds
A. E. Simons
A. H. W. Smith
H. W. Smith
H. W. J. Smith
R. J. Smith
T. W. Spain
E. J. Spooner
P. M. Stephens
S. L. Stone
G. E. Swan
N. A. Swan
J. V. Symmons
W. S. Thomas
J. Tomlinson
A. R. Turner
H. Turner
E. D. Vercoe
F. Warr
H. E. Warriner
H. Watson
J. S. Whish
C. J. White
W. H. White
S. Whiteside
H. Willis
H. Wilson
J. A. Wilson
C. W. Windibank
J. J. Worledge
R. Worthington
J. E. Wrigley
W. H. Yates
H. G. Yearsley
A. H. Youlton

SALONICA PANTOMIME

Men serving in Salonica will remember the Pantomime 'Aladdin' which was given on Christmas Day, 1916, and repeated on several occasions. After the War it was presented for many years at the Guildhall School of Music in London and served as a basis of a re-union for men who served in that part of the globe. Mr. R. W. Rayner, who was with the 1st Surrey Yeomanry, gave a description of it at the time and sent over a programme.

ALADDIN

A PANTOMIME IN TWO ACTS

By Members of the Field Ambulance

ACT I.—A Well in Macedonia

ACT II.—Outside Mrs. Twankey's House in Bal-Bluma

CAST

MRS. TWANKEY, a Woman in Macedonia	*Private S. Bramall*
ALADDIN, Her Son	*Sergeant C. H. D. Pratt*
GINGER, His Mule	*Private S. S. Cox and Corporal F. C. Ross*
OROSOI AND STAIN, Slaves of the Lamp	*Privates E. James and O. Bunyard*
ABANAZAR, a Terrible Turk	*Sergeant F. Izod*
PANKAKOS, N.C.O. in Abanazar's Harem	*Private A. Skinner*
FATIMA, Favourite Wife of Abanazar	*Private H. Sharpe*
KOPRIVA, GODIVA, PATELLA, BANANA, CASCARA — Other Wives	*Privates J. Brown, E. Harris, W. Blaiklock, T. Kay, C. Williams*
MAJOR TWANKEY	*Sergeant Yates*
SERGEANT BLUSTER	*Private L. E. Shepherd*
PRIVATE BERTIE BAYSWATER	*Private G. G. Horrocks*
PRIVATES PERCY PIMLICO, WILLIE WANDSWORTH — Pals of Bertie Bayswater	*Privates H. Sharpe and C. N. Williams*
MISS KITTY FRASER, a girl from Blighty	*Corporal E. J. Dillon*

Soldiers, Tortoises, Muleteers.

The theatre was made out of three large marquees pitched on a slope.

The scenery was painted by the men in the Division and the footlights were oil and acetylene lamps. At least eight or nine Prudential men were there including Sergt. Pratt and Sergt. Izod whose names are in the programme—also Corpl. Davies who had charge of the band and songs and also played a violin solo before the pantomime. The costumes were 'scrounged' locally. Corpl. G. H. Davies, an accomplished musician, possessed a violin which deserves mention. The violin was sent out to him at Ypres and accompanied him through the War. It survived all kinds of disasters. He stuck it together with glue at a French farmhouse after the Battle of Loos, and managed to save it in Macedonia when torrential rain washed away the tents. He gave pleasure to soldiers wherever he went with his music, but this was not the only side to his activities. He was awarded the Military Medal in 1917 for displaying the greatest initiative and bravery for the treatment and evacuation of patients under heavy fire.

THE WAZIRISTAN CAMPAIGN

Mr. J. R. Gawen writing from the Murree Hills in December, 1917, says:

'I don't know whether the people in England have heard of the Waziristan Field Force. The campaign had as its object the recovery from the tribesmen of a few thousand Service rifles which they had raided from the Frontier forts during the early part of the year. We started out at the beginning of June, and for over a month advanced through the rocky and barren mountains. The Mahsuds are considered the cleverest hill-fighters on the Frontier and they fought up to their reputation. They could retire up a mountain-side faster than we could come down, and they were absolutely invisible at 100 yards. We would attack a hill under heavy fire, but on reaching the summit there would not be a Mahsud in sight. But from the top of another and higher hill down would come a volley of miscellaneous bullets, some of them an inch in circumference, and all soft-nosed. We would be fighting and picketing from 5 a.m. to 5 p.m., and would then set to work to build a breastwork round the camp. We would finish work about 10 p.m., and consider ourselves lucky if we got a night in our blanket free from attacks and snipers.

'We were at it for over a month and when at last we got within striking distance of their capital and holy city of Khaniguram and the Mahsuds decided that discretion was the better part of valour, we were just about at the end of our endurance. We made a permanent camp at Boji-Khel while peace conferences were held, and what with bad water and the privations they had gone through, over a third of the battalion were down with dysentery in less than a week.

'As soon as possible we moved to a healthier spot, Mazal, to await the arrival of the disputed rifles. After a week there the monsoon rains broke among the hills, and, living as we were, wet through day and night, and fever almost visible in the air, it was no wonder that hardly a white man in the force escaped malaria. I myself was sent back to India with a combination of diseases of which ague, malaria and jaundice were the worst.

'The battalion reached its depot at Lahore just 200 strong out of the 817 who started.'

Others whom we have traced as having served in this campaign are :

S. H. Akhurst
A. R. Combeer
E. Hack
C. E. Hammond
A. J. Harris
A. P. Howlett

THE FALL OF JERUSALEM

The taking of Jerusalem was of outstanding importance in the history of the War. It gave proof to the world of the *morale* of the British Army and the British Nation. Sir Edmund Allenby had captured Beersheba and Gaza and pushed on towards Jerusalem. Turks and Germans alike made frantic efforts to save it. But by 9th December, 1917, Jerusalem was isolated and on Tuesday, 11th December, Sir Edmund Allenby entered by the Jaffa Gate.

Mr. F. B. Barren was amongst the first to mount guard when Sir Edmund Allenby made his entry into the city and Mr. A. V. Beechener was Sergeant of one of the earliest guards on the gates. He tells us : 'The guardroom was at the Jaffa Gate and there were posts at all the others. Visiting these posts during the night, traversing the narrow overhanging and unlighted streets and alleys of the old city was an interesting but rather eerie experience.' Mr. W. Mortimer as Captain of the Guard held the keys of the city for one day.

Mr. N. A. Swan was amongst those to enter Jerusalem on the day it fell. On the 27th December, when the Turks counter-attacked north of Jerusalem, Mr. Swan was wounded.

Others who took part in the capture of Jerusalem or in subsequent operations in this area are :

W. H. Adley
A. G. Amphlett
H. J. G. Back
H. C. Bateman
R. Charters
A. E. Cooke
A. J. Dalton
F. B. Davies
C. R. Dixon
G. H. Drain
J. E. Evans
H. M. Fieldgate
A. L. Hitchin
W. C. Hogge
E. H. King
T. E. W. Knight
A. E. Lavers
J. H. Lee
C. E. McLoughlin
W. Mortimer
F. Murgatroyd
A. Nicholson
T. E. Pain
H. E. Parker
R. A. Pedler
B. W. Penford
A. W. Plant
J. Ritchie
G. Scriven
A. H. W. Smith
W. H. Stevenson
C. H. Stockbridge
A. H. Tandy
G. G. Thomson
F. L. Woodgate

THE RUSSIAN EXPEDITIONARY FORCES

As is generally the case with the majority of events connected with Russia the doings of the Allied Forces which served in that country during the War are clouded in mystery.

Forces comprised of British, French, Italian, Serbian and American contingents were landed at Vladivostock in the Far East and at Archangel and Murmansk in the North. Both by reason of their numbers and their proximity to the main sphere of operations the forces in the North doubtless had a more direct influence upon subsequent events. The fact that the port of Murmansk is normally open to shipping throughout the year lent colour to the suggestion that the object was to prevent the enemy from utilizing that part of the coast for submarine bases, but it is more probable that the principal purpose was to create uncertainty in the minds of the opposing commanders, and to divert a measure of their attention from the Western Front.

Owing to the collapse of the rouble, financial experts accompanied the forces to deal with questions of currency and exchange. As far as the Archangel and Murmansk armies were concerned, special problems were also presented in the matter of food and clothing, and advice in these matters was given on the spot by the late Sir Ernest Shackleton who had been specially attached to the expedition for that purpose.

Such military operations as were undertaken were hampered by the varying loyalties of the population following the internal political upheaval, but casualties were fortunately light. Nevertheless, few who served in the Northerly regions will forget the other danger which threatened in the winter months as a result of the long absence of sunshine—the effects of mental depression.

Once again, however, the general adaptability of the British soldier was proved. He was expected to overcome unusual climatic conditions (for which he was paid an extra 6*d.* a day), but he attained also in a surprisingly short time a creditable degree of skill in the use of skis.

The first landings were made in the summer of 1918, but owing to the intricacy of the situation, final evacuation was not secured until over a year later.

A number of the Staff visited Russia and had varying experiences.

Amongst them were the following: C. J. Avenell, A. W. Beer, E. J. Bond, W. F. Boston, J. E. Brindley, B. H. Cooper, W. H. Cunningham, A. T. Goodier, T. W. Gowlett, C. J. Hedger, S. P. Hess, G. L. Hill, A. B. Maclean, D. S. McLeish, F. W. G. Osborne, F. Raybould, R. W. Rayner, J. T. Roberts, P. Rocker, H. W. Shaw, J. N. Shine, L. H. G. Thomas, W. L. Tokeley, W. Wallace, W. H. White, and W. J. Woodman.

Mr. D. S. McLeish, describing the conditions on the River Dwina front, mentions that the shell-fire and bombing were insignificant compared with experiences in France, but other conditions were terrible. The weather was severe, 20° to 30° below zero being usual in the winter. (Mr. L. H. G. Thomas did sentry duty when the temperature was 34° below zero, an experience he never forgot.) There were long lines of communication on which the journey took from ten days to a fortnight when the river was frozen. In mid-winter there was no daylight and in mid-summer no night.

Mr. E. J. Bond had the pleasure of seeing the voluntary surrender of two Bolshevik generals. There had been a victory over the Bolsheviks and the generals surrendered as they were liable to be shot by their own authorities for their failure to annihilate Mr. Bond and his friends.

Mr. S. P. Hess had an exciting experience in the village of Murmansk. A house-to-house search was made by his unit for arms. He was ordered into a large hut where twenty rifles were found, which the Russians said they had permission from the authorities to keep. A man was sent back to headquarters to confirm this and Mr. Hess was left on guard. After being in the hut for about two hours one of the sergeants came rushing in. They had forgotten Mr. Hess and left without him. After a roll call, however, it was discovered that he was missing, but the authorities had forgotten where they had posted him. It was thought he must have been murdered and a search was organized for his body. It was in this search that the sergeant found him.

Mr. F. W. G. Osborne, who spent three years and nine months in Russia, had the unusual experience of a mutiny on a troopship in the Black Sea. The troops ordered the Captain to stop the ship and on the following morning General Milne arrived with two warships. The General came on board and a conference was held lasting for four hours. The troops were assured they were not going to fight the Russians and the ship proceeded on its way.

Mr. B. H. Cooper's ship was lying in harbour when General Petlura attacked and took Odessa. On the following evening Mr. Cooper went ashore and describes the scene after the battle :

'Armed pickets, on guard at each street corner, eyed me with suspicion, shepherding me along their respective beats, and carefully "turning me over" from one to the other. They were not very fierce-looking warriors, those Ukrainian peasant boys, but I began to wonder whether they would acquiesce in my returning on board.

'On December 19th the Russian Volunteer Army rallied its forces, and, with a combination of strategy and machine-guns, drove back Petlura's troops. On December 20th the city was normal again : the Diriba Skaia crowded with light-hearted promenaders, Fanconi's overflowing, and the opera in full swing. Shattered window-panes, chipped and damaged buildings, bloodstains, and a ruined railway station constituted the only evidence that yesterday the streets had been scenes of strife.'

PRUDENTIAL WOMEN IN THE WAR

THE lot of the wartime generation of girls was no less tragic than that of the men, for whilst comparatively few of them were asked to give their lives, all, or nearly all, lost something of their youth, which they never quite regained.

Under the strain of personal anxiety and privation Prudential women threw themselves into war work. Many of them not only did their work at the office but also spent weary vigils at stations in all weathers waiting for the arrival of hospital trains. They dressed wounds and cooked and scrubbed in the hospitals. They were not infrequently in a hospital full of wounded during an air raid. All these things and more Prudential women did and endured. Most of them gave their services through the Red Cross.

As far back as 1910 six Voluntary Aid Detachments for women were formed and classes in First Aid and Home Nursing were held in the office by Colonel Broome Giles. When proficiency in both subjects was attained the women were enrolled as members of Immobile Detachments and were given uniforms. Field Days for First Aid and Stretcher work were held and the V.A.D.s were entertained by both Sir Thomas Dewey and Sir William Lancaster who lent them their grounds.

Certain members were called up for duty outside the Mansion House for the Lord Mayor's Show in 1911, and this duty has continued to the present time.

When the War broke out regular parties went to the Guildhall and the Mansion House to deal with the vast quantities of hospital equipment which was collected for Red Cross work.

Two hospitals were opened in the city: Fishmongers' Hall for officers and later the City of London V.A. Hospital in Finsbury Square for other ranks.

Both these hospitals were staffed as far as possible by Prudential detachments. To begin with the detachments dealt with laundry and kitchen work and then worked in the wards for day and night duties.

Both hospitals, being in the heart of the city, were involved in all the air raids on London.

Finsbury Square Hospital was considered unsafe during air raids, and directly the command 'Action Stations' was given all helpless cases were brought down to the ground floor and those who could be moved were transferred to the National Provincial Bank building, then under construction in Finsbury Square. After the air raid on Whit-Sunday night, 1918, the 'All Clear' signal was given, but as the men were being taken back to the ward the warning came again and it was necessary to return to the 'dug-outs'. Many had just come off a transport from Salonica and were suffering from malaria, but the alarms and excursions had no ill-effects and their temperatures were normal in the morning. When the King George V Hospital was opened in Great Stamford Street, several Prudential members were asked to join the staff, and it was from this hospital that Miss G. E. Lewis, Miss G. M. S. Boom and Miss I. Paul went overseas.

The work at this hospital was particularly interesting as British prisoners of war who had been exchanged were sent there before returning to their homes. The patients were mostly disabled and the work of the German doctors was inspected by all the leading doctors and surgeons in London. Complicated operations had often been performed without anæsthetics as these were unobtainable in Germany.

In all, the following ladies were released by the Company for the duration of the War :

4 V.A.s served overseas.
14 V.A.s served in London.
2 W.A.A.C.s served overseas.
1 Land Girl served in England.

Considerably more than 100 V.A.s were released for three or six months at a time for hospital duty. One of the members paid a foreign barber to teach her his trade. When she was proficient she visited a hospital each morning before coming to the office to shave and trim the hair of the helpless patients. Her work was greatly appreciated as barbers were scarce in those days.

When the Ambulance Column was reorganized towards the end of the War it was customary for one or two women V.A.s to go out on the calls. Many of the Lady Staff, although not officially released from their office duties, worked on week-end and night-shifts at canteens and did war work of all kinds. Some even took regular turns at the arsenals and undertook really heavy work making munitions.

INDIVIDUAL EXPERIENCES

Here in brief are the experiences of some of our ladies :

Miss J. E. Balfour joined the Voluntary Aid Detachment in 1910. Mobilized in 1915 she served as a Commandant, being finally demobilized in 1918. She was awarded the M.B.E. In a letter Miss Balfour described life at a Red Cross Hospital. After giving particulars of the staff at the hospital where she was on duty, Miss Balfour paid a tribute to the younger V.A.s who worked under her supervision :

'. . . Those who were not old enough or not sufficiently qualified for actual nursing worked under my supervision. I had the pleasure of working with more than 20 of these members, and I cannot speak too highly of their cheerful willingness to do whatever was required of them. Three came on duty from 7.30 a.m. to 1.30, and three from 1.30 to 8.30 or 8.45 p.m.

'Our duties were to see to the setting of tables for meals, the clearing away afterwards and the washing up of glass, silver, cups and saucers ; the keeping in order of the dining-rooms generally, and incidentally, a great many other things. The dining-rooms are so arranged that the staff-room—where the Officers, Sisters and Nurses have their meals—the Patients' room and the Orderlies' room lead into one another.

'Perhaps if I give you our time-table you will be better able to realize the amount of work we had to do.

7.30 a.m.—Resident Orderlies' breakfast. My nurses had to be on duty in time to make the tea for this meal.
8.0—Breakfast for Officers and Night Orderlies.
8.30—Night Sisters' dinner, two Day Orderlies' breakfast.
10 to 10.15—Cocoa and hot milk for Day Sisters and Nurses.
11.45—Matron's coffee.
12.0—Hot milk for Night Sisters.

12.15 p.m.—Patients' dinner.
1 p.m.—Officers', Sisters' and Orderlies' dinner.
1.30—Second dinner for Sisters, Nurses and Orderlies.
4.0—Patients' and Masseuse's tea ; and also special trays for Matron, Doctor, any member of the Committee, or Civil Administrator.
4.30—Sisters', Nurses' and Orderlies' tea.
5.0—Second tea for Sisters, Nurses and Orderlies.
6.30—Patients' supper.
7.15—Officers' dinner.
8.0—Night Sisters' breakfast and Orderlies' supper.
8.30—Sisters' supper. After that we began to think it was nearly time to go home.

'Our patients frequently had entertainments, which added somewhat to our work, for the dining-room was turned into a concert hall. Tables had to be cleared and put away before 5 p.m. ; the entertainment usually continued until 6.20 or 6.30 p.m. ; then, as smoking was allowed, the floor had to be swept ; tables were then replaced and laid ready for supper.

'The men, who were mostly convalescent and able to take their meals in the dining-room, said very little about themselves. They were usually very shy until they had been in hospital for two or three weeks, and even then were more likely to talk of their homes than what they had gone through. It was most pathetic to see many of them crippled for life in some way or other, and yet generally very cheerful. One's own troubles and trials grew small by comparison.

'Doubtless the ambition of every member of the Red Cross Society is nursing, but it is necessary that some should undertake work similar to the pantry work described above ; by this means even the youngest and least well-equipped member has ample scope for "doing her bit". It cannot be called, nor do we consider it, menial work. Surely nothing that is done for the men who have risked their lives for the sake of our homes and our country can be considered menial work, even if it is only washing up the mugs out of which they drink !'

Miss F. A. Bird joined the Women's Auxiliary Army Corps in July, 1917, and served in Etaples, France, as forewoman. She was demobilized in December, 1919.

Miss G. M. S. Boom was mobilized in the Voluntary Aid Detachment in 1914. At first she was on duty at Fishmongers' Hall. In June, 1915, she went to King George V Hospital which had just been opened. In December of the same year she was sent to Palermo, Sicily, to work in a Red Cross hospital at the Villa Egica which had been opened and financed by Lord Monson and the Hon. G. Beaumont for men who had been wounded in the evacuation of the Dardanelles. In March, 1916, the hospital closed. In the following June Miss Boom was sent to No. 7 Stationary Hospital with the British Expeditionary Force in France. In November, 1917, the Hospital Unit was rushed with the 1st Division to Italy at the time of the Italian retreat, Miss Boom going to No. 11 General Hospital at Genoa, where she remained until demobilized.

Miss C. M. Butcher joined the Voluntary Aid Detachment in May, 1915. She spent three months at Finsbury Square Hospital and the remainder of the time at Fishmongers' Hall.

Miss O. Chinnery joined the Voluntary Aid Detachment and served at Fishmongers' Hall. From December, 1915, until May, 1919, she served at the City of London Red Cross Hospital.

Miss Margaret Fidler joined the Red Cross in 1910. In May, 1915, she was serving with the Voluntary Aid Detachment, being sent to Oxford with the first batch of V.A.s, where she nursed officers and, later, Colonials at Somerville College. In June, 1917, she went to Etaples, France, to No. 56 (Territorial) Hospital. The hospital was bombed continuously throughout the summer of 1918. In August, 1918, Miss Fidler was transferred to No. 4 General Hospital at Dannes Camiers.

Miss M. Fitch joined the Voluntary Aid Detachment in 1910. In 1915 she went to the King George V Hospital, which was the largest hospital for wounded soldiers in London at the time. She became a Commandant in 1918 and was awarded the Red Cross Efficiency Stripe.

Miss D. K. Guest joined Queen Mary's Auxiliary Army Corps on 29th July, 1917, and served as Private, Forewoman Clerk, Assistant Administrator and finally Deputy Administrator. Whilst in France she was within the sound of guns in the Ypres Salient and was frequently bombed in night and day raids. On one occasion five bombs dropped in the courtyard over which she worked. Fortunately, however, they only caused confusion and cuts and bruises. On another occasion an aerial torpedo went through the house next to her billet and buried itself in the foundations.

Miss B. Haycraft joined the Voluntary Aid Detachment in 1910. From 1915 to 1919 she served at the City of London Red Cross Hospital, also eighteen months at Finsbury Square and occasionally at Fishmongers' Hall.

Miss M. Henderson joined the Red Cross in 1908. During the War she was at King George V Hospital and on night duty at Fishmongers' Hall for three months. She was awarded two Proficiency Medals and bars.

Miss C. I. Joyce joined the Women's Land Army in May, 1917, serving until November, 1918, at Willesborough, near Ashford, Kent.

Miss G. E. Lewis was on duty as a Quartermaster at Fishmongers' Hall in 1914. In 1915 she continued at King George V Hospital. She went to France in 1916 serving at No. 25 General Hospital at Hardelot. Later she served at No. 10 Hospital at St. Omer, No. 53 General Hospital at Wimille, and eventually at No. 46 Hospital at Etaples.

Miss E. G. Lowenstam joined the Red Cross and in 1914 was on service at Fishmongers' Hall. From April, 1915, until June, 1919, she was on duty at King George V Hospital.

In 1914 Miss A. Macnab was mobilized with the Voluntary Aid Detachment. After two months at Fishmongers' Hall she proceeded to King George V Hospital and was resident there for the period of the War. This hospital consisted of 2,000 beds and was run partly by the Red Cross and partly by the War Office. After the Armistice the hospital served as a base for prisoners from Germany who were incapacitated by wounds or sickness. As it was by the river—which was a guide to the Zeppelins—there was always great anxiety during air-raids, but no harm was ever done, although after Zeppelin raids the roof of the hospital was covered with shrapnel. Miss Macnab was in every air-raid, both night and day. In May, 1919, she left the service having been mentioned in despatches, gained all nursing stripes and awarded the Royal Red Cross.

Miss C. G. A. Naylor joined the Voluntary Aid Detachment in 1914 and served as a V.A. in the 124th Essex Detachment at the Walthamstow General Hospital, and also at Hale End Red Cross Hospital, E.4 on week-end duty. She was called up by the 2nd City of London to go to the Finsbury Square Red Cross Hospital in 1916 and was appointed for the duration of the War. On one occasion a bomb was dropped on the corner of Chiswell Street and shrapnel came in the windows of the hospital. This hospital was a general dressing-station.

Miss G. M. Sparling joined the Voluntary Aid Detachment in September, 1914, and worked at Fishmongers' Hall for the duration of the War—for the first nine months as a cook, and as a V.A.D. nurse for the remainder of the time. She was on duty when the present Queen Elizabeth—then Lady Elizabeth Bowes-Lyon—visited her brother Lieut. Bowes-Lyon who was a patient in the ward in which Miss Sparling worked. Miss Sparling holds several certificates for service, one of which is signed by Queen Alexandra.

Miss G. F. Taylor joined the Voluntary Aid Detachment. During 1915 she was on night and day duty at Fishmongers' Hall. Sometimes she did day duty in the laundry. From 1916 to 1918 she worked at King George V Hospital, also on day and night duty.

Miss G. M. Wensley joined the Voluntary Aid Detachment, 6th City of London. She was mobilized in 1914 and served as a Commandant at Fishmongers' Hall until demobilized in February, 1919.

PEACE

At the Annual Meeting of the Prudential Clerks Society held on January 6th, 1919, the Chairman, Mr. A. C. Thompson put a resolution expressing '. . . admiration and grateful appreciation of the undying deeds, sufferings, and self-sacrifice of the 1,058 members who are serving or have served with His Majesty's Forces; and deepest sorrow for the loss of 156 gallant lives which have been nobly laid down in a righteous cause, and whose names will ever be kept by all in lasting fraternal remembrance.'

Mr. Thompson, in the course of his speech proposing the resolution said: 'It tells the story simply as it should be told, because I think that one great feature is that, quietly and simply, without any boasting and without any fuss, they have gone to their task, whether in the Flanders Lines or wherever their duty has called them. They have endured their period of training and the hardships which have followed; they have bled for the cause, and in many cases they have died, and we have here to record amongst our own number 156 gallant lives. It would have been impossible for this War to have been won unless these and other men had come forward at the call of duty. They have done it willingly for the cause of Freedom, and they have had no thought of reward. I think they would have found a very sufficient reward in the knowledge that they and others of our countrymen were collectively writing another glorious page in the history of this nation. . . .'

MR. A. C. THOMPSON ADDRESSES SOME OF THOSE RETURNED FROM THE WAR

On the 20th February, 1919, Mr. A. C. Thompson addressed a body of the staff who had returned from the War and resumed their civilian duties. In the course of his speech he said:

'. . . You probably represent all branches of the Service. Some of you have been in the midst of very great danger, others have not had that experience. Most of you have suffered as a result of the fighting, some have been prisoners of war; you have all had the common liability to be sent anywhere, to do anything that might be required. Some of you have come back the worse for your experience, physically and mentally, and it will take some time for you to recover to the full. On behalf of all of us I offer you a very hearty welcome on your return . . .

With reference to the London Ambulance Column, Mr. Thompson said that their work had been very valuable to men who had been on Active Service and that the story of the war-work of the staff would be incomplete without reference to the London Ambulance Column.

AFTER THE ARMISTICE

It was many months before our men were finally demobilized and not a few went with the Army of Occupation into Germany and remained there until October, 1919. We have been able to trace the following:

D. Allan
W. H. Angel
J. W. Attree
H. S. Bishop
J. A. Bissett
J. W. Bolderson
A. H. Brown
F. H. Bugden
G. B. Burton
H. G. Carter
S. L. Carter
F. Collins
A. J. Cooper
C. F. Cox
C. Cuthbert
A. J. Dack
F. B. Davies
R. Davies
J. T. Dawes
V. M. Deakins
C. H. Dell
H. P. Denton
A. M. Dowell
C. Eccles
L. F. Edwards
W. L. Edwards
R. W. Emery
L. Evans
W. M. Evans
J. G. Feugill
S. Gawthorne
E. A. H. Goldfinch
W. J. Gough
L. H. Hall
W. L. Hall
F. G. Hancock
F. J. Harris
J. B. Haslem
W. A. J. Hill
J. W. Hillman
J. H. Holmes
C. J. Horner
G. Howard
H. J. Huckle
F. C. Hughes
W. G. James
E. M. Jones
C. R. Justice
C. F. Ladbrook
W. Lambert
C. B. L. Langley
G. F. Ledgard
J. R. Lewis
L. Libretto
W. Lifford
R. Lillie
S. J. Manley
A. Mann
C. G. Marshall
G. A. McNaughton
M. H. Molyneux
H. V. C. Moody
F. Morcom
R. F. Morris
G. Murray
G. O. Parish

W. G. Parry
L. W. Payton
H. Proctor
H. C. Rand
F. Rasor
A. J. Rawlins
H. A. Read
H. L. Richardson
F. J. Roberts
T. W. Robinson
G. G. Rush
S. R. S. Ryder
C. Sampson
A. C. L. Serff
W. R. Shalders
W. Sherdley
J. Slade
H. C. Small
D. C. Smith
H. F. Smith
R. M. Smith
F. T. Stephens
R. C. Stevenson
W. A. Tackley
A. E. Tombleson
W. Trimmer
A. J. Tucker
J. Turner
C. R. Upson
W. J. Wakefield
J. Walker
M. M. Wilkins
S. E. Williams
W. A. Williams
E. J. M. Wilson
L. Wilson
F. L. Woodgate
H. G. Yearsley

Mr. T. W. Butler was with the Army of Occupation in the Dardanelles.

Mr. H. G. Bailey served in Austria after the Armistice and Mr. L. Hanks in the Austrian Tyrol.

Mr. C. H. D. Pratt was with the Army of Occupation in Gallipoli and Constantinople.

Mr. H. S. Bishop, who was with the Army of Occupation in Cologne, was billeted in a Baron's house. The German coachman who belonged to the establishment used to drive King Edward VII when he went to Wiesbaden. He was very proud of this fact and had a framed photograph of King Edward being driven by him and also a medal presented to him by the King.

Mr. H. Andrews stayed in Germany several months until peace was signed and was selected to proceed to France. His duties were to clear a portion of the devastated area of all ammunition in order that the French farmers could return to the land. He had to inspect ammunition to see if it was safe to travel and was also in charge of five hundred Chinese and a few Indians for the purpose of labour. Eventually he formed an ammunition dump of many thousands of tons at Boyelles, near Arras.

After the Armistice Mr. E. J. Barraclough was stationed at different towns on the Nile Delta to keep order among Egyptian rioters.

Mr. T. Neuenschwander, who manned the first gun fired in the War (see page 9), was present at a Sea Service Review in the Thames. Most of the steamship lines were represented, the Merchant Service having done such good service for the country. Nine cutters from the Royal Navy formed the Guard of Honour to the King, Mr. Neuenschwander being one of the crew.

After a guarantee letter had been received by Mr. A. H. Fleman's Commanding Officer he was sent to 250th (Divisional) Employment Company where his demobilization papers were signed by Captain V. G. Taylor, now Divisional Manager D/G Divisions.

Whilst at Ripon, Mr. G. H. Gilbert acted as a demobilization officer and discharged a man aged 69 who had joined up in 1914, under a false age.

THE WAR MEMORIAL

The ceremony of the unveiling and dedication of the War Memorial took place in the courtyard of Chief Office, on Thursday, 2nd March, 1922.

It was a bright March morning. The great quadrangle was filled with relatives, friends and colleagues of the fallen, and every window of the building was occupied. The Memorial was draped with the Union Jack and the White Ensign. Two soldiers and two sailors stood one at each corner. Drawn up at the side was a guard of honour of Prudential men under the command of Lieut.-Colonel A. H. Windsor, C.M.G. There were two pipers of the London Scottish, also members of the staff, buglers of the Coldstream Guards, a row of seated disabled men, a cordon of ex-soldiers and sailors of all ranks and a number of ladies of the staff who had seen service overseas.

At 11 o'clock the President, Sir Thomas Dewey, Bart., inspected the guard of honour, and took up his position, with Mr. A. C. Thompson, Chairman of the Company, and the Rector of St. Andrew's, Holborn, the Rev. E. C. Bedford, upon the platform especially erected near the Memorial.

After the hymn "O, God, our help in ages past," had been sung there followed prayers offered by the Rector, and then Mr. A. C. Thompson addressed the assembly :

'We have come here remembering with thankfulness, not unmixed with lawful pride, the wonderful response made by our colleagues, men of the Prudential staff, who responded to the call addressed to them in the name of our country. A call to offer themselves, and all that life held for them, in order that we as a nation might retain the freedom for which our forefathers fought and bled. This beautiful Memorial will serve in particular as a perpetual remembrance of that wonderful patriotism manifested by our men,

9161, of whom were actually enrolled for active service in the Great War. More particularly today we desire to give expression to our love for those whose names are actually inscribed on this Memorial. . . . Seven hundred and ninety, some of them our relatives, all of them our friends and colleagues, who laid down their lives for God and King and for Country.

'I think that most of us who are members of the great Prudential family share in our hearts the belief that the ties which unite us—Directors, Officers and Staff—are closer and more affectionate in their nature, and our spirit of comradeship is more fully developed than is usual amongst people who are associated together mainly in the pursuit of commercial ends. The part played by the Company in the War, whether in the enrolment of men for service, or in direct assistance to the Government, and various other ways, or in caring for the dependants of those serving ; or in proper consideration for the demobilized men ; that record is known to us all and appreciated by us all. It was a time for common sacrifice which, though differing very greatly in degree, was yet directed to the accomplishment of a common purpose ; and so its effect has been to knit us all yet more closely together, and we appreciate the ceremony for which we have assembled in a common purpose and in a kindred spirit.

'The grief and the pride with which today our hearts are full are alike concerned with our domestic circle, and we feel it is especially in keeping with the family traditions that the unveiling of this Memorial to Prudential men should be undertaken by the President of the Company, our greatly esteemed friend and leader, Sir Thomas Dewey.'

Then followed the unveiling ceremony. With the words—'I now unveil this Memorial to the glory of God and to the undying memory of our brave fellow-workers in the Prudential' Sir Thomas Dewey touched a cord and the draped flags slipped to the ground, revealing the Memorial in all its beauty.

Sir Thomas Dewey then returned to the platform and said :

'The Memorial, my dear friends, is in grateful remembrance of that splendid staff of Prudential men who in the prime of life so readily responded to the call of duty and gave their lives for their King and Country in the Great War. The recorded names will ever remain an abiding memorial of that glorious band of heroes and their gallantry and unselfish devotion will ever be an inspiration to us all.'

The General Manager, Sir Joseph Burn, placing a wreath on the War Memorial, 1938

The Memorial was then dedicated by the Rector in lasting memory of those of the Company who had offered their lives for World Freedom and International Righteousness.

The hymn, ' O Valiant Hearts ', was sung, and the pipers played the lament, ' Flowers of the Forest '. Then came the Last Post, sounded by the buglers of the Guards.

After the singing of the National Anthem, Mr. A. C. Thompson introduced the sculptor, Mr. F. V. Blundstone, R.B.S., to the assembly, and publicly expressed the thanks of all to him for the beautiful Memorial which he had designed.

The wreath in memory of the dead was then placed on the Memorial by Sir Thomas Dewey on behalf of himself, the staff and relatives.

Sir Thomas Dewey, Bart., died on the 13th July, 1926, and Mr. A. C. Thompson on the 9th November, 1928. Every year since the unveiling either the Chairman of the Company or the General Manager has placed a wreath upon the War Memorial at the conclusion of the Two Minutes Silence on Armistice Day.

The names of all those who fought in the War are honoured by the generation to which they belong.

Twenty years is a long time, and as each Armistice Day comes round the number of those who remember the dead grows fewer. In another twenty years there will be very few indeed. A new generation will stand silently about the Memorial wondering, no doubt, what sort of men were these whose names are engraved on the bronze tablets.

Will this story have any significance for that new generation? Sometimes the men who spent their youth in the shadow of death may well wonder.

> And year by year our memory fades from all the circle of the hills.

We hope that this book will perpetuate the memory of those of the war-time generation of Prudential men and women and also that those coming after will find inspiration in these simple tales of civilians turned soldiers, and the courage and devotion which animated them.

INDEX

(Of the names of members of the staff to whom specific reference is made)

www.ingramcontent.com/pod-product-compliance
Ingram Content Group UK Ltd.
Pitfield, Milton Keynes, MK11 3LW, UK
UKHW051128260726
13967UKWH00010B/2918